RELIGIOUS HOUSES OF WINCHESTER

AN OVERVIEW

By Stephen Old

**TIMELINE HISTORY AND ARCHAEOLOGY
(HAMPSHIRE)**

Religious Houses of Winchester

Published by
Timeline History and Archaeology (Hampshire)
27 Ashley Gardens, Chandlers Ford, Eastleigh SO53 2JH
timelinehistoryhampshire@gmail.com

British Library Cataloguing in Publication Data.
A CIP Record for this title is available from the British Library

ISBN 978-1-8381838-6-8

Front Cover Photograph: St Cross Hospital ©Stephen Old
Back Cover photograph: Winchester Cathedral © Stephen Old

Printed by Sarsen Press, 22 Hyde St, Winchester, SO23 7DR

*Whilst every care has been taken to ensure the accuracy of the
information contained in this book, the publisher disclaims
responsibility for any mistakes which may have been inadvertently
included.*

Contents

Foreword 4

Acknowledgments...5

Introduction 6

Chapter 1 – Definitions and Background Information 8

Definitions...8

Christian Religious Monastic Orders 16

Christian Military Religious Orders 21

Chapter 2 – Winchester's Medieval Christian Establishments....24

Male Christian Houses 24

The House Of The Austin Friars Of Winchester....................25

The House Of The Dominicans Of Winchester 27

The Priory Of St. Swithun, Winchester................................34

New Minster, Or The Abbey Of Hyde 50

The House Of The Franciscans Of Winchester 65

The House Of The Carmelites Of Winchester 69

Female Christian Houses 69

Nunnaminster, Or The Abbey Of St. Mary, Winchester 69

The Harley Manuscripts 79

Chapter 3 – Christian Hospitals 81

The Hospital Of St. Cross, Near Winchester 81

The Hospital Of St. Mary Magdalen, Winchester 92

The Hospital Of St. John Baptist, Winchester 100

The Sustern/Sustren Spital 106

Christ's Hospital 107

Chapter 4 – Christian Colleges 108

The College Of St. Elizabeth, Winchester................................ 108

St. Mary's College or Winchester College/School.................... 114

Chapter 5 Winchester's Jewish past **127**

    Early Medieval Jewish Winchester **127**

    Archaeology and Architecture **133**

    Definitions **135**

Chapter 6 Pre-Christian Winchester **138**

    Iron Age **138**

    Roman Period **139**

Chapter 7 The Black Death and Winchester's Clergy **142**

Chapter 8 Wrapping Up **145**

Bibliography **146**

Foreword

When you live in or near to a city like Winchester in the county of Hampshire, Great Britain, it is very easy to ignore the history that is there, right in front of your eyes. We see the streets and the buildings and they are familiar to us, so they bear no further examination or thought, we take them for granted. I suppose it is the same with any place we visit on a regular basis, we become "history blind".

There are many publications on the history of Winchester and its environs, but they tend to fall into one of two types, either very academic and sometimes a bit heavy going, or the tourist style that gives the bare minimum in the way facts but lots of pictures. I have enjoyed both types in the past and they both serve a useful purpose. By writing this book, I am trying to provide a source document for those interested in Winchester's religious past, but also provide it in a way that is easy to read and accessible. I will not only look into the history of Christian religious sites in Winchester, but also the sites of other religions, like Judaism or Paganism, as these religions also had a marked influence on the development of the City of Winchester.

As well as the written history of Winchester, found in the many documents that survive, I will also delve into the archaeology, as this expands and explains the reality of the times when Winchester was one of the top religious centres in the whole of England, but which has remained buried, until revealed, during one of the many excavations which have taken place city wide, when the opportunity has arisen. For this I will draw on the work done by the Winchester Excavations Committee (WEC) and the Winchester Archaeological Rescue Group (WARG-Now called Winchester Archaeology and Local History) who have been very active in Winchester over the last 50 years. I am not an academic in the sense that I work in academia, although I was a part time lecturer in archaeology on a leisure course at Barton Peveril and then Eastleigh College, I do, however, have a deep interest in the subject.

Acknowledgments

The research was mainly carried out using online facilities and books that I have in my collection. On line, the main source was "British History Online" and especially *"A History of the County of Hampshire: Volume 2, edited by H Arthur Doubleday and William Page (London 1903)"*. The Many books I have consulted include those written or edited by Professor Martin Biddle CBE, FBA, FSA, Patrick Ottaway, Ken Qualmann, Richard Whinney, Graham Scobie and many others. For basic background information on the subject I have used the books "Abbeys and Priories" by Glyn Coppack and the "Sutton Companion to Churches" by Stephen Friar. There is a full bibliography at the end of the book.

I have used the, as yet unpublished, records of the excavations carried out by WARG (Winchester Archaeology and Local History Group), at the time of writing I have the roles of the society's Chair.

I have also used the noters from a talk given to WARG by Dr John Merriman with his kind permission.

All photographs, unless otherwise stated were taken by myself and have been cropped and adjusted to fit the text.

Introduction

Winchester has a very long history as a place of habitation and religious observance, from before the Iron Age, as a Roman settlement, an Anglo-Saxon settlement, through the Normans where religion also played a key role through to the modern day. Like most modern cities, which have been subject to development and change over the centuries, a lot of what we see in Winchester at ground or even first floor level, is not the full picture. There is a great deal of history hidden behind a slapped-on façade and hidden behind an attempt to make the building appear more modern and commodious. These only become exposed for further examination when building work takes place for some reason.

It is not just the High Street, with the new shop fronts and display windows, this is also the same with domestic houses and religious buildings. There are many "Georgian" fronted houses that hide a much early building underneath and behind. There are also many religious buildings that have been "Modernised" in the past, had a new shell erected covering the original building, or at least an earlier version. This is especially the case when the buildings use has changed from being the home of a religious community to the home of a rich family.

Winchester was once the home for many religious communities of all Christian denominations and persuasions as well as other non-Christian religions. A great many of these were done away with at the time of King Henry the Eighth (1491-1547) and the "Dissolution of the Monasteries", ably assisted by Thomas Cromwell (1485-1540), when the Abbeys, Friaries, Priories, Convents and Monasteries were gradually closed down and stripped of their assets, wealth and power. This supreme act of vandalism, because that is what many people think it was, effectively destroyed centuries of supportive communities that the common man relied on. It was not just the fabric of the buildings that went but also the local economy, the local charitable organisations and the civic administration that were greatly affected. The buildings, however, were very much a part of the equation. Their grandeur and their imposing nature can only now be guessed at and glimpsed in the archaeology. England lost a great deal of important architectural heritage with this single act, possibly more than was lost during the second world war.

I will be looking at the religious houses of Winchester from Anglo-Saxon origin through to the dissolution and beyond, but I will also briefly look at those that have their base in the history before the Anglo-Saxons. I will concentrate mainly on the ones that have survived to this day but will also go through the historical stories of houses that are no longer in existence, but written and archaeological records exist for them.

I will be using a variety of sources and texts but will mainly take what is written in the book "A History of the County of Hampshire: Volume 2, edited by H Arthur Doubleday and William Page (London, 1903)". I will, where it helps the text and does not change the basic meaning, alter some words to modern equivalents. This should make the reading of this book an easier and more pleasant experience.

Happy reading.

Steve Old

Chapter 1 – Definitions and Background Information

Definitions

There are many terms, when talking about religious houses, that can be confusing and where their meaning and use has changed over the years. Here I have put together a list of these terms, in alphabetical order, and given the meaning that would have been attached to them in times past. Some have gone out of use entirely but others have had their meaning expanded or corrupted. This is not an exhaustive list as I am sure, even in this text, other words and terms will crop up.

Abbey – An abbey is a type of monastery used by members of a religious order under the governance of an abbot or abbess. Abbeys provide a complex of buildings and land for religious activities, work, and housing of Christian monks and nuns.

Abbott/Abbess – Abbot is an ecclesiastical title given to the male or female head of a monastery in various western religious traditions, including Christianity. The office may also be given as an honorary title to a clergyman who is not the head of a monastery. The female equivalent is abbess.

Aisle – From the Latin for "Wing", this is a lateral extension of a nave from which it is divided by an arcade, normally of pillars. An aisle was intended to add extra space for the congregation.

Almonry – Monastic buildings often included an Almonry from which alms were distributed.

Almshouse – An Almshouse is charitable housing provided to people in a particular community. They are often targeted at the poor of a locality and at those from certain forms of previous employment, or their widows, and at elderly people who can no longer pay rent, and are generally maintained by a charity or the trustees of a bequest. Almshouses were originally formed as extensions of the church system and were later adapted by local officials and authorities.

Ambulatory – A covered walkway providing a covered route between buildings on a monastic site, perhaps between the Frater and the Church, or Dorter and the Chapter House. Also, this term is used for semi-circular aisle enclosing an apsidal presbytery or chapel.

Apse – A polygonal or semi-circular recess characteristic of the early basilicas of the Christian church, they were usually at the East end of the church and they were replaced in the 12th century by a square feature.

Arcade – A range of arches resting on piers or columns. The term is used to describe the arched division between the nave of a church and its aisles.

Balneary – In a monastic complex this was a room set aside for the residents to bathe and perform their ablutions. Not all monastic sites would have had one of these and they were more common on mainland Europe.

Baptistery – A room or building next to a church, used for baptism.

Calefactory – Also known as the warming house was a very important room or building in a medieval monastery. It was here that a communal fire was kept so that the monks could warm themselves after long hours of study in the usually unheated cloister or after doing other work, outside in all weathers.

Canon – **A** canon is a member of certain bodies subject to an ecclesiastical rule. Originally, a canon was a cleric living with others in a clergy house or, later, in one of the houses within the precinct of, or close to, a cathedral or other major church and conducting his life according to the customary discipline or rules of the church. This way of life grew common in the eighth century. In the eleventh century, some churches required clergy thus living together to adopt the rule first proposed by Saint Augustine that they renounce private wealth. Those who embraced this change were known as Augustinians or Canons Regular, whilst those who did not were known as secular canons.

Canonry – The office of a canon; a benefice or prebend in a cathedral or collegiate church.

Cellarium – The store house for the monastery where food and drink would be stored in cool conditions to help preservation, normally at underground level.

Chancel – This is the part of a church near the altar, reserved for the clergy and choir, and typically separated from the nave by steps or a screen or both.

Chantry – A chantry may refer to one of two meanings of the term. Firstly, it could mean the prayers and liturgy in the Christian church reserved for the dead as part of the search for atonement for sins committed during their life. It might include the mass and by extension, the endowment left for the purpose of the continuance of prayers and liturgy. It could be called a type of "trust fund" established during the pre-Reformation medieval era in England for the purpose of employing one or more priests to sing a stipulated number of services for the benefit of the soul of a specified deceased person, usually the donor who had established the chantry in his will. There could be a stipulated period of time immediately following her/his death. It was believed such masses might help atone for misdeeds and with mercy enable the soul to be granted eternal peace in the presence of God. Chantries were commonly established in England and were endowed with lands, rents from specified properties and other assets by the donor, usually in his will. The income from these assets maintained the "chantry" priest.

Chapel – A chapel is a Christian place of prayer and worship that is usually relatively small, and is distinguished from a church. The term has several senses. Firstly, smaller spaces inside a church that have their own altar are often called chapels; the Lady chapel is a common type of these. Secondly, a chapel is a place of worship, sometimes non-denominational, that is part of a building or complex with some other main purpose, such as a school, college, hospital, palace or large aristocratic house, castle, barracks, prison, funeral home, cemetery, airport, or a military or commercial ship. Thirdly, chapels are small places of worship, built as satellite sites by a church or monastery, for example in remote areas; these are often called a chapel of ease. A feature of all these types is that often no clergy were permanently resident or specifically attached to the chapel.

Chapter House/Chapterhouse – This is a meeting room where the whole community would meet to pray or discuss issues, often centrally located within the complex.

Choir – see Quire.

Claustral – relating to the cloister and the associated buildings attached and accessed via the cloister.

Clerestory – This is the upper part of the nave, choir, and transepts of a large church, containing a series of windows. This was to allow natural light into the church.

Cloister – A cloister (from Latin claustrum, "enclosure") is a covered walk, open gallery, or open arcade running along the walls of buildings and forming a quadrangle or garth. Usually placed against the south facing wall. It was seen as a barrier between the inside monastic world and the outside working people.

College – A body of clergy living together and supported by a foundation. A building used for an educational or religious purpose.

Convent – A convent is either a community of priests, religious brothers, religious sisters, monks or nuns; or the building used by the community, particularly in the Catholic Church, Lutheran churches, and the Anglican Communion. Usually now used for a female religious community.

Dorter – This is the dormitory of the monastic complex where the brothers would have slept communally. Most were later converted to individual cells but the name remained.

Frater – This is another word for the refectory or dining room of a monastery or abbey. This is where the residents would gather at set times to eat and drink between the other set parts of the daily routine like praying and working.

Friar – A friar is a brother and a member of one of the mendicant orders founded in the twelfth or thirteenth century; the term distinguishes the mendicants' itinerant apostolic character, exercised broadly under the jurisdiction of a superior general, from the older monastic orders' allegiance to a single monastery formalized by their vow of stability. The most significant orders of friars are the Dominicans, Franciscans, Augustinians and Carmelites.

Friary – a community or monastery of friars, usually a group of monastic and domestic buildings that supported the life and activities of the Friars and the local community.

Hospital – Their name indicated their primary function; it was derived from the Latin word hospitalis, meaning being concerned with hospites, or guests, and guests were defined as any persons who needed shelter. Some of the hospitals were, therefore, erected for the use of pilgrims and other travellers; others were really Almshouses, intended chiefly for the poor and the aged.

Hospitium – This was a lodging house for travellers especially one maintained by a religious order. They were also called Hospices. They were normally located in the outer precinct of a monastery or abbey and were often administered independent from the house.

Infirmary – Also called the Farmery, this is a place for the care of the infirm, sick, or injured. It was set up like a monastic site in miniature with its own Dorter, Frater, kitchens and chapel.

Lavabo – A fixture or area set aside for people to wash their hands before entering the refectory or chapel. Some of these were very ornately decorated and had room for many users at the same time, like the one a Wenlock Abbey in Shropshire.

Lavatorium – This is another word for Lavabo but is often applied to a room for washing rather than just a fitting.

Layman – A member of a religious community or church that has not been ordained or taken holy orders. Committed to the community but free from most of the self-imposed restrictions.

Minster – Minster is an honorific title given to particular churches in England, most notably York Minster, Westminster Abbey in London and Southwell Minster in Nottinghamshire. The term minster is first found in royal foundation charters of the 7th century, when it designated any settlement of clergy living a communal life and endowed by charter with the obligation of maintaining the daily office of prayer. Widespread in 10th-century Anglo-Saxon England, minsters declined in importance with the systematic introduction of parishes and parish churches from the 11th century onwards. It continued as a title of dignity in later medieval England, for instances where a cathedral, monastery, collegiate church or parish church had originated with an Anglo-Saxon foundation. Eventually a minster came to refer more generally to "any large or important church, especially a collegiate or cathedral church". In the 21st century, the Church of England has designated additional minsters by bestowing the status on existing parish churches.

Misericorde – The room in a monastery used by monks who have been granted a dispensation from normal monastic rules including fasting. The term is also applied to a seat in a church, often called "pity" seats that allowed the brothers, who were infirm, to have some support during long services. The word translates as "mercy".

Monastery – A monastery is a building or complex of buildings comprising the domestic quarters and workplaces of monastics, monks or nuns, whether living in communities or alone. A monastery generally includes a place reserved for prayer which may be a chapel, church, or temple, and may also serve as an oratory, or in the case of communities anything from a single building housing only one senior and two or three junior monks or nuns, to vast complexes and estates housing tens or hundreds. A monastery complex typically comprises a number of buildings which include a church, dormitory, cloister, refectory, library, balneary and infirmary. Depending on the location, the monastic order and the occupation of its inhabitants, the complex may also include a wide range of buildings that facilitate self-sufficiency and service to the community. These may include a hospice, a school, and a range of agricultural and manufacturing buildings such as a barn, a forge, or a brewery.

Monk – A monk is a person who practices religious asceticism by monastic living, either alone or with any number of other monks. A monk may be a person who decides to dedicate his life to serving all other living beings, or to be an ascetic who voluntarily chooses to leave mainstream society and live his or her life in prayer and contemplation. The concept is ancient and can be seen in many religions and in philosophy.

Nave – This is the central part of a church building, intended to accommodate most of the congregation. In traditional Western churches it is rectangular, separated from the chancel by a step or rail, and from adjacent aisles by pillars. It stretches from the entrance on the west wall to the chancel.

Necessarium – another word for the Reredorter or communal latrine which would be attached or close to the Dorter.

Night Stair – A stairway and passage that was used by the monks when called to prayer in the early hours. It is placed as a direct route from the Dorter or dormitory to the church in order to make the trip short and distraction free.

Nun – A nun is a member of a religious community of women, typically one living under vows of poverty, chastity, and obedience. She may have decided to dedicate her life to serving all other living beings, or she might be an ascetic who voluntarily chose to leave mainstream society and live her life in prayer and contemplation in a monastery or convent.

Porch – Unlike Cathedrals and Abbey churches that have great west doorways, most churches have a door on the south wall. This was usually protected from the elements by a porch.

Presbytery – The eastern part of a church chancel beyond the choir (quire) and also known as the sanctuary, sanctum, sacrarium or tabernacle.

Prior – Prior, derived from the Latin for "earlier or first", is an ecclesiastical title for a superior, usually lower in rank than an abbot or abbess. Its earlier generic usage referred to any monastic superior.

Priory – A priory is a monastery of men or women under religious vows that is headed by a prior or prioress. Priories may be houses of mendicant friars or nuns, or monasteries of monks or nuns. Houses of canons regular and canonesses regular also use this term, the alternative being "canonry".

Quire – An alternative spelling for choir, the place where services are sung. Choirs are commonly in the chancel, at the east end of the church, generally separated from the nave by the chancel arch and possibly a screen.

Reredorter – The reredorter or necessarium was a communal latrine found in mediaeval monasteries in Western Europe and later also in some New World monasteries. It was normally attached to the south end or the east side of the monks' dormitory or "dorter" on the east of the main cloister with seats arranged on the first floor of the building allowing direct access from the dormitory.

Reredos – This is an ornamental screen covering the wall at the back of an altar.

Rood – This is a cross or crucifix symbolizing the cross on which Jesus Christ died; specifically : a large crucifix on a beam or screen at the entrance to the chancel of a church. The Rood screen is a screen that incorporates or supports the rood.

Sacristy – A room in a church or chapel set aside for the keeping of the orders sacred vessels and vestments and where the clergy puts on their vestments. In older buildings this is often by the side of the high alter and in some monastic sites it is a separate building.

Sanctuary – The sanctuary is the most holy part of a religious building and contains the altar and is contained within the presbytery.

Scriptorium – Literally "a place for writing", is commonly used to refer to a room in medieval European monasteries devoted to the writing, copying and illuminating of manuscripts commonly handled by monastic scribes. However, lay scribes and illuminators from outside the monastery also assisted the clerical scribes. The room would normally be placed so that natural light could illuminate the pages they were working on.

Spital – A charitable house to receive and care for sick people, later distinguished from a hospital as being especially for those of a low class or meagre financial means.

Transept – In a cross-shaped church, either of the two parts forming the arms of the cross shape, projecting at right angles from the nave. These are normally to the North and South of the church.

Vestry – See Sacristy.

Christian Religious Monastic Orders

There are many religious orders that have used the United Kingdom as home at some time in the past. The ones I have listed here have at some point had a presence locally but not necessarily in Winchester, but it gives you an idea of the breadth of religious observance during the middle ages.

Benedictine – Benedictine, member of the Order of Saint Benedict (O.S.B.), member of any of the confederated congregations of monks, lay brothers, and nuns who follow the rule of life of St. Benedict (*c.* 480–*c.* 547) and who are spiritual descendants of the traditional monastics of the early medieval centuries in Italy and Gaul. The Benedictines, strictly speaking, do not constitute a single religious order, because each monastery is autonomous. St. Benedict wrote his rule, the so-called Benedictine Rule, *c.* 535–540 with his own abbey of Montecassino in mind. The rule, which spread slowly in Italy and Gaul, provided a complete directory for both the government and the spiritual and material well-being of a monastery by carefully integrating prayer, manual labour, and study into a well-rounded daily routine. By the 7th century the rule had been applied to women, as nuns, whose patroness was deemed St. Scholastica, sister of St. Benedict.

Carmelite – These were one of the four great mendicant orders (those orders whose corporate as well as personal poverty made it necessary for them to beg for alms) of the Roman Catholic Church, dating to the Middle Ages. The origin of the order can be traced to Mount Carmel in north western Israel, where a number of devout men, apparently former pilgrims and Crusaders, established themselves near the traditional fountain of Elijah in about 1155. Their rule was written between 1206 and 1214 by St. Albert, Latin patriarch of Jerusalem, and approved in 1226 by Pope Honorius III. The monks hoped to continue on Mount Carmel the way of life of the prophet Elijah, whom early Christian writers depicted as the founder of monasticism.

Franciscan – The Franciscans are a group of related mendicant religious orders within the Catholic Church, founded in 1209 by Saint Francis of Assisi. These orders include the Order of Friars Minor, the Order of Saint Clare, and the Third Order of Saint Francis. They adhere to the teachings and spiritual disciplines of the founder and of his main associates and followers, such as Clare of Assisi, Anthony of Padua, and Elizabeth of Hungary.

Augustinian – Augustinians are members of Christian religious orders that follow the Rule of Saint Augustine, written in about 400 CE by Augustine of Hippo. There are two distinct types of Augustinians in Catholic religious orders dating back to the 12th–13th centuries:

- Several orders of friars who live a mixed religious life of contemplation and apostolic ministry. The largest and most familiar is the Order of Saint Augustine (OSA), founded in 1244 and originally known as the Hermits of Saint Augustine (OESA). They are commonly known as the Austin Friars in England. Two other orders, the Order of Augustinian Recollects and the Discalced Augustinians, were once part of the OSA under a single prior general. The Recollects, founded in 1588 as a reform movement in Spain, became autonomous in 1612. The Discalced's became an independent congregation in 1592, and were raised to the status of a separate mendicant order in 1610.

- Various congregations of Canons Regular also follow the Rule of Saint Augustine, embrace the evangelical counsels and lead a semi-monastic life, while remaining committed to pastoral care appropriate to their primary vocation as priests. They generally form one large community which might serve parishes in the vicinity, and are organized into autonomous congregations.

There are also some Anglican religious orders created in the 19th century that follow Augustine's rule. These are composed only of women in several different communities of Augustinian nuns.

Cluniacs – Cluniacs were Benedictine monks from the monastery of Cluny (Burgundy) France, founded by William, duke of Aquitaine, in 909. Cluny was a centre of reformed observance, laying great stress on the rule, the liturgy, and freedom from lay (and, indeed, episcopal) control. Under the leadership of its early abbots, especially Odo (927–42), Odilo (994–1048), and Hugh (1049–1109), Cluny enjoyed considerable prosperity, and exercised a wide influence on monastic reform elsewhere in Europe, while an increasing number of monasteries were taken under Cluniac control, or adopted Cluniac observances. The order was extremely centralized, Cluny's abbot possessed autocratic powers within the order, and other Cluniac foundations or 'priories' were subordinate to Cluny, where their monks made profession. The Cluniacs were closely involved with the papal reform movement of the late 11th cent. And Pope Urban II (1088–99) was himself a Cluniac. Under Hugh's abbacy, Cluny reached the height of its prestige as a spiritual and cultural centre, famous for its music and rebuilt abbey church, which, when consecrated in 1131–2, was perhaps the grandest in western Europe. The first English Cluniac priory was founded by William de Warenne in 1077 near his castle at Lewes. His, the largest community, was joined by some 30 more, most being founded in the late 11th and 12th centuries. Though initially subject to Cluny's authority and hence regarded as 'alien priories' and liable to sequestration during the Anglo-French wars, most purchased national identity as 'denizens" (a foreigner allowed certain rights in their adopted country).

Cistercians – Cistercian, byname White Monk or Bernardine, member of a Roman Catholic monastic order that was founded in 1098 and named after the original establishment at Cîteaux (Latin: Cistercium), a locality in Burgundy, near Dijon, France. The order's founders, led by St. Robert of Molesme, were a group of Benedictine monks from the abbey of Molesme who were dissatisfied with the relaxed observance of their abbey and desired to live a solitary life under the guidance of the strictest interpretation of the Rule of St. Benedict. Robert was succceded by St. Alberic and then by St. Stephen Harding, who proved to be the real organizer of the Cistercian rule and order. The new regulations demanded severe asceticism; they rejected all feudal revenues and reintroduced manual labour for monks, making it a principal feature of their life. Communities of nuns adopting the Cistercian customs were founded as early as 1120–30, but they were excluded from the order until about 1200, when the nuns began to be directed, spiritually and materially, by the White Monks.

Carthusians – The Carthusians, also known as the Order of Carthusians (Latin: *Ordo Cartusiensis*), are an enclosed religious order of the Roman Catholic Church. The order was founded by Bruno of Cologne in 1084 and includes both monks and nuns. The order has its own rule, called the *Statutes*, and their life combines both eremitical and cenobitic monasticism. The motto of the Carthusians is *Stat crux dum volvitur orbis*, Latin for "The Cross is steady while the world is turning."

The name *Carthusian* is derived from the Chartreuse Mountains in the French Pre-alps: Saint Bruno built his first hermitage in a valley in these mountains. These names were adapted to the English *charterhouse*, meaning a Carthusian monastery. Today, there are 23 charterhouses, 18 for monks and 5 for nuns. The alcoholic cordial Chartreuse has been produced by the monks of Grande Chartreuse since 1737, which gave rise to the name of the colour.

Premonstratensians – Premonstratensian, byname White Canon, or Norbertine, member of Order of the Canons Regular of Prémontré, abbreviation O. Praem., a Roman Catholic religious order founded in 1120 by St. Norbert of Xanten, who, with 13 companions, established a monastery at Prémontré, France. The order combines the contemplative with the active religious life and in the 12th century provided a link between the strictly contemplative life of the monks of the preceding ages and the more active life of the friars of the 13th century. The Premonstratensians followed the monastic rule of life of

St. Augustine, but their supplementary statutes, which were greatly influenced by Cistercian ideals in both the manner of life and the government of the order, made their life one of great austerity. The order was approved by Rome in 1126 and quickly spread over western Europe. Later, after its austerity had been relaxed, reforms were undertaken and a number of more or less independent congregations were created. The order was nearly destroyed by the French Revolution.

Trinitarians – Trinitarian, member of Order of the Most Holy Trinity for the Redemption of Captives (O.SS.T.), a Roman Catholic order of men founded in France in 1198 by St. John of Matha to free Christian slaves from captivity under the Muslims in the Middle East, North Africa, and Spain. St. Felix of Valois has been traditionally considered as cofounder, but recent critics have questioned his existence. The order had its own rule, distinguished for its austerity, and devoted one-third of its possessions and revenues to the liberation of slaves. No accurate figure for the number of captives ransomed can be given, but it has been estimated that the total was as high as 140,000. Because slavery is no longer an international problem, the order now devotes itself to teaching, giving missions, and serving in parishes, hospitals, and prisons. The order is said to have numbered 5,000 members in 1240, but, by the end of the Middle Ages, a decline had set in, and various reforms were attempted during the 16th century. In 1597 a reform called the Barefooted (Discalced) Trinitarians was initiated in Spain by Juan Bautista of the Immaculate Conception; this became a distinct order and is the only surviving branch of the Trinitarians.

Dominicans – Dominican, byname Black Friar, member of the Order of Friars Preachers, also called Order of Preachers (O.P.), one of the four great mendicant orders of the Roman Catholic Church, founded by St. Dominic in 1215. Its members include friars, nuns, active sisters, and lay Dominicans. From the beginning the order has been a synthesis of the contemplative life and the active ministry. The members live a communal life, and a careful balance is maintained between democratically constituted chapters, or legislative assemblies, and strong but elected superiors. In contrast to the monastic orders that predated it, the Dominican order was not a collection of autonomous houses; it was an army of priests, organized in provinces under a master general and ready to go wherever they were needed. The individual belonged to the order, not to any one house, and could be sent anywhere at any time about its business; this innovation has served as a model for many subsequent bodies.

Norbertine – see Premonstratensians.

Basilian – Founded in 356, these monks and nuns follow the Rule of Basil the Great. This order is primarily Eastern Orthodox. Nuns work in schools, hospitals, and charitable organizations. There is no evidence of them having a presence in Winchester, but as an early order, it is possible that there was some representation for which records no longer exist.

Christian Military Religious Orders

A military order is a Christian religious society of knights. The original military orders were the Knights Templar, the Knights Hospitaller, the Order of Saint James, the Order of Calatrava, and the Teutonic Knights. They arose in the Middle Ages in association with the Crusades, both in the Holy Land and in the Iberian peninsula; their members being dedicated to the protection of pilgrims and the defence of the Crusader states. They are the predecessors of chivalric orders. There are two types of military order, international and nation specific.

Most members of military orders were laymen who took religious vows, such as of poverty, obedience, and chastity, according to monastic ideals. The orders owned houses titled commanderies all over Europe and they had a hierarchical structure of leadership with the grand master being at the top.

The Knights Templar, the largest and most influential of the military orders, was suppressed in the early fourteenth century; only a handful of orders were established and recognized afterwards. However, some persisted longer in their original functions, such as the Sovereign Military Order of Malta and the Order of Saint John, the respective Catholic and Protestant successors of the Knights Hospitaller. Those military orders that survive today have evolved into purely honorific or ceremonial orders or else into charitable foundations.

Order of the Holy Sepulchre – Originally an "association" of knights who guarded the Church of the Holy Sepulchre under the jurisdiction of the kings of Jerusalem. In 1113, they became consubstantial with the Canons of the Holy Sepulchre after their recognition by Pope Paschal II, as a military branch, Militi Sancti Sepulcri; after 1291, the Knighthood was awarded to prominent pilgrims by the Custos of the Holy Land. Reorganised as the Sacred and Military Order of the Holy Sepulchre in 1496 by Pope Alexander VI. Reorganised again by Pope Pius IX with the residential restoration of the Latin Patriarchate of Jerusalem in 1847. Known as the Equestrian Order of the Holy Sepulchre of Jerusalem since 1931.

Knights Hospitaller – Founded between 1099 and 1113 by Gerard Thom in Jerusalem as protectors and suppliers of resources to the Latin Kingdom of Jerusalem. The head of the order was a Grand Master from 1113 to 1607, then a Prince from 1607 to 1630 and a Cardinal from 1630 onwards. Officially it still remains a Christian order, with a Catholic successor, the Sovereign Military Order of Malta, and a Protestant successor, the Order of Saint John, both of whom mutually recognise one another.

Knights Templar – The Knight Templar were founded in 1118 by Bernard of Clairvaux and Hugues de Payen. They were, perhaps, the most powerful and influential of the Jerusalem Knights The Knights Templar order was reconstituted in Portugal after the Templars were abolished on 22 March 1312 by the papal bull, Vox in excelso, issued by Pope Clement V. King Dinis I of Portugal created the Order of Christ (Portugal) in 1317 for those knights who survived their trials throughout Europe and was officially founded in 1319. The property of the Templars was transferred to the Knights Hospitaller except in the Kingdoms of Castile, Aragon, and Portugal. In effect, causing the dissolution of the Templars by the rival order.

Thus when being recognized, the Pope allowing only the "Order Of Christ" a Portuguese order and its Papal branch "Supreme Order of

Christ" can claim to have any descent from the Templars, which is now used for Honorary State merits in Portugal and preserved as such.

Teutonic Knights – Also called the "Order of Brothers of the German House of Saint Mary in Jerusalem". Founded in 1190 at Acre in the Holy Land (at the time called the Latin kingdom of Jerusalem). It was founded to aid Christians on their pilgrimages and provide hospitals. The main stem of the Teutonic Knights converted into a purely Catholic religious order in 1929.

The Bailiwick of Utrecht of the Teutonic Order separated from the Roman Catholic mainstem during the time of the Reformation and continues as a Protestant chivalric order.

Chapter 2 – Winchester's Medieval Christian Establishments

From Anglo-Saxon times Winchester was a seat of Christian learning and a place of pilgrimage with several saints having their burial here as well as the burials of many of the royal family and their entourage. This continued with the advent of the Norman period and the following Plantagenets. In fact, it was not until the Tudor period that things changed dramatically with the coming of the dissolution of the Monasteries'.

Winchester was the home of many religious houses and the monastic orders represented were quite wide and encompassed nearly every version in existence during these times.

Life in these houses was hard and the rules strict, for both monks and nuns, but they were safe and secure, which was more than can be said for life in general, even for the rich. Politics was also very prominent within the hierarchy of these houses and with their various benefactors, lie could become very complicated and your tenure could be fragile.

Winchester had seven known Christian religious houses within the city bounds or just outside. Housing monks, nuns and lay people in separate establishments but originally some would have been mixed sites, though this later changed and was frowned upon.

Male Christian Houses

In medieval times it was very much a male dominated society and the majority of the religious orders that made their home in the Winchester city area were mainly populated by males, other than their domestic servants. This is not to say that women were excluded, but they tended to have their establishments in more rural areas. In previous Saxon period, many of the religious establishments catered for both male and female inhabitants, the community living separately but together on the same campus.

The House Of The Austin Friars Of Winchester

The establishment of the Austin friars, or friars-hermits of St. Augustine at Winchester in the reign of Edward I is well documented. In 1302, Geoffrey Spiring of Fareham gave to the Austin friars a messuage (Dwelling) in the suburb of Winchester for the enlargement of their area and in 1313, Hugh Tripacy granted them a plot of land, 12 perches long by 6 perches wide, adjoining their dwelling place, for further enlargement. Bishop Sandale (1316-20) ordained three friars from the Austin house at Winchester; and his successor, Bishop Asserio (1320-3), the same number.

In July, 1328, the grant of the Bishop of Winchester to the Austin friars of the lane called Sevenetwychene, in the south suburb without the walls contiguous to their house, for the enlargement of the site, was confirmed by the king. The site was located outside the city walls just south of the south gate on what is now St cross road. In June, 1343, Pope Clement VI. instructed the Bishop of Winchester to grant licence to the prior and Austin friars of Winchester to accept a manse in the city given them by Oliver Bohun, knight, and Margaret his wife with King Edward's licence, and thither to transfer themselves, and build a church and necessary offices; their place without Southgate being in a dangerous, lone and unfit site. The bishop, however, for certain reasons, opposed this removal; but in May, 1346, the prior received the pope's sanction to at once proceed to the new site without any longer waiting for the consent of the diocesan. Milner says that the site of this house after its removal was opposite St. Michael's church, in a close called College Mead.

The following is the meagre inventory of the goods of the friars taken at the time of the dissolution of the house.

"Md this stuffe under wryttyn ys praysed by Mayster Burkyn, alderman of Wynchester and Mayster Knyght at the mayorys assygnacion by ye syght of the kynges vysytor under the lorde privye seal for ye kynges grace the whyche longyd to the austen frearys, that is to say: iiij great candelstykes ij small, a stop (sic)

and copper crosse about an C and an halffe, vjs. viijd.; Wyll'm Alen berebrewar axythe for bere; iiij aulter clothys, ijs. iiijd.; ij payntyd clothys, xd.; a sensor, xyjd.; iiij antepaynys, xxd.; a surpples and a rochet, viijd.; vj coupys, xiijs. iiijd.; ij towellys, ijd.; a myeter, jd.; ij small crossys coveryd with sylver, iijs. iiyd.; a banner clothe, viijd.; ij quysshons, xijd.; iiij corporasys with the casys, xvjd.; a sute of grene wantynge an albe, vs.; viij vestymenttes with ther albes, xxs.; a crosse and a laten baason and a paxe, iiijs.; ij deske clothys, xd.; viij lent clothys, iijs. viijd.; iij chests, ijs.; a paxse, ijd.; iij fether beedes and a bolster, ixs.; ij coverys, vjd.; iiij brasse pottes and ij panys, xvjs.; ij cobyrons a trevet a pothooke a hoke eyaryn (iron), xviijd.; a bason, ij coverys, ij borddes, xxd. Summa vli. vijs. ixd."

Below is an attempt to translate the above text, though some areas I have left as I could find no common replacement word.

"Mind this stuff underwritten is appraised by Master Burkin, alderman of Winchester and master Knight at the mayors assignation by the sight of the Kings visitor under the lord privy seal for the kings grace to which belonged to the Austin Friars, that is to say 4 great candlesticks, 2 small, a stop and copper cross about a C and a half, William Allen Beer Brewer access for beer; 4 altar cloths, 2 painted cloths; a sensor; 4 antipains, a surplus and a rochet; 6 cups 2 towels, a mitre, 2 small crosses covered in silver, a banner cloth, 2 cushions, 4 corporasys with the cases, a suit of green wantage and long white vestment, 8 vestments with their long white tunics, a cross and a laten basin and a paxe (Wooden Tablet with image of Christ or the Virgin Mary etc.), 2 desk clothes, 8 lent clothes, 3 chests, a paxse, 3 feather beds and a bolster, 2 covers, 4 brass pots and 2 pans, 2 cob irons a trivet a pothook a hook iron."

There were debts on the house to the amount of 27s (shillings).

In archaeological surveys and excavations between 2007 and 2010 by Southern Archaeological Services, the Friary was located on the premises of 19 St Cross Road and St Michael's Gardens, with some of the layout being determined. The church chancel and nave was typically elongated and of a size to accommodate a large congregation. On the north side of the western end there was evidence that there might have been a chantry chapel. To the south of the church were the cloisters and other buildings, with the site of the chapter house being determined.

As with many such sites, burials were found within the complex of buildings. One deep grave in the centre of the chancel was accompanied by a Papal Bull (decree). About 30 others were found in the chapter house, within the northern cloister walk and north of the church. Evidence of further burials to the north of the church was found with grave cuts in Friary Gardens.

The House Of The Dominicans Of Winchester

At the second general chapter of his Order held at Bologna in May, 1221, St. Dominic decided to send thirteen friars to England to establish the Dominicans there. This first missionary band of friar-preachers journeyed in the train of Bishop Peter des Roches, who was then returning to his diocese. The bishop first endeavoured, in 1225, to establish these Dominicans at Portsmouth; but the project fell through, probably owing to his absence from his diocese from 1226 till 1230. The date of their establishment at Winchester is somewhat uncertain, but it was between 1231 and 1234. There appear to be no surviving papers from the founding to corroborate these dates. The Dominicans were called the "Black Friars" due to the black cappa they wore.

According to Matthew Paris, it was a Dominican friar from Winchester who preached the crusade in Winchester in 1234, when Richard, Earl of Cornwall, the king's brother, and many other magnates took the cross. The site assigned for their convent was in the High Street, near the Eastgate, with the river Itchen on the east and Busket Street on the west. The ground round the house, excluding the buildings, was about 2½ acres, for which they paid the Crown the yearly rent of 3s. 5d.

Henry III. was their munificent patron throughout his reign, particularly in helping them with their buildings. In 1235, he gave forty oaks for building out of the forest of Bere; in 1236, ten oaks out of the same forest for fuel; in 1239, 100s., and in 1240, 20 marks for building; in 1246, 15 marks for the works; in 1256, ten oaks to finish the frater; in 1260, six oaks fit for timber towards their church, then in progress; in 1261, six oaks fit for timber out of Pamber Forest (near Tadley, North Hampshire), which the bailiffs of Southampton were to deliver; in 1262, ten oaks; in 1265, twelve oaks fit for timber; in 1269 ten good oaks for the repair and ornamenting of the church; in 1270, six good oaks for ceiling the church, then approaching completion; and in 1271, ten more oaks, five from Portchester Forest and five from Pamber, for the construction of the infirmary.

The King further bestowed on the Winchester Dominicans other gifts in kind, the record of which affords information as to their number. In 1239, each of the twenty eight friars received from Henry III. a pair of shoes and four ells of cloth for tunics. Like gifts of clothing were made for the next five years, when the friars numbered thirty-one. In 1261 they had a royal grant of £10 to buy winter clothing and shoes. Cartloads of wood or dead oaks for fuel were frequently granted them by the Crown, and on one occasion a tun of wine.

In 1266 licence was granted by the Crown for the friars to enclose a small lane which was adjacent to their site.

The church of the friars-preachers of Winchester was dedicated to St. Katharine, the patroness of the Order. The buildings when finished could accommodate from forty to fifty of the friars. Edward I. did much for the house, but now that it was finished there was not the same necessity for royal bounty. He gave them on several occasions leafless or dead oaks for fuel, and in 1298 ten oaks fit for timber out of the Forest of Bere.

When the king visited Winchester in 1302, he gave this convent an alms of 38s. for three days' food. When Edward II. visited the city on 29 April, 1325, he gave to the forty-six Dominican friars an alms of 15s.

6d. for a day's food, being at the rate of 4d. a head. Edward III. on his arrival in Winchester on 23 November, 1331, found thirty-six friars in the convent, and rendered an alms of 12s. for the like purpose.

When the provincial chapter was held at Winchester in 1259, Henry III. gave the friars 100s. towards their expenses. In 1315 a provincial chapter was again held at Winchester, when Edward gave 100s. for three days' food for himself, and the like amount both for his queen and for his son Edward. When the Order assembled here on 16 February, 1339, Edward III. gave the like sum of £15; and on 21 October he diverted to the same purpose the £20 which the Crown usually bestowed on the general chapter, as the chapter of that year was held at Clermont, France, with which country England was then at war.

Some information has already been given with regard to episcopal licences to the Dominicans and other friars for preaching and acting as penitentiaries. It may be of interest to note that the episcopal registers show that during the episcopacy of Bishop Asserio (1320-3) three acolytes, two sub-deacons, six deacons and six priests were ordained from this convent; that during Wykeham's rule of the diocese (1367-1404) two acolytes, one deacon and ten priests were ordained; and that from 1511 to 1527 thirty-six received orders from this house.

Various friars of the Winchester convent were distinguished in their Order. Brother Matthew was prior or warden of Winchester in 1242, and also English provincial. Brother William of Southampton, who died about 1278, was head of the Winchester house, and elected provincial in 1272. He was a distinguished theological writer. Robert de Bromyard, who was licensed to preach in the diocese in 1300, was doubtless prior of the Winchester convent, for he was elected provincial in 1304; he was also penitentiary of the diocese from 1307 until his death in 1310. Nicholas de Stratton, D.D., who was provincial from 1306 to 1311, and also diocesan penitentiary, was a Winchester prior. William de Horleye was prior in 1326. Thomas de Lisle, who was ordained in St. Elizabeth's chapel in 1322, was the next prior. He was employed in an embassy to the papal court in 1340-1, and was consecrated Bishop of Ely on 24 July, 1345, at Avignon, where he died in exile in 1361. William Alton, born at Alton, Hants, a renowned preacher and writer, a doctor of Paris University who flourished about 1350, was probably of the Winchester convent. John Payne was prior in 1373. The Court Rolls of Winchester name as prior John Derle, 1377 and 1387; Nicholas Monk, 1404 to 1426; and Walter Alton, 1455.

James Cosyn, B.D., who was prior in the time of Henry VIII., adopted the most extreme tenets of the reformers. He preached a sermon from St. John xvi. 23, in the parish church of 'Chusel' (Chessel?) on 27 February, 1536, of which the following are passages: 'If thou put an whole stoup of holy water upon thy head, and another stoup of other water upon thy head, the one shall do thee as much good as the other in avoiding of any sin. As much other bread of thine own blessing shall do thee as much good as so much holy bread. And as for confession, I will not counsel thee to go to any priest to be confessed, for thou mayest as well confess thyself to a layman, thy Christian brother, as to a priest, for no bishop or priest have any power to assoil any man of any sin. And I myself have shriven a woman this day here in this church, but I did not assoil her, no, I will never assoil none.'

Whereupon this 'soul-murderer,' as the vicar of Stoke styled him, was arrested and indicted for heresy, and committed by the sheriff to the custody of Dr. Edmund Steward, the chancellor of Winchester. But on 31 March William Basing, prior of St. Swithun, wrote to Thomas Cromwell beseeching his favour 'to a friar named Cosyn, wrongfully vexed in these parts.' Soon after a testimonial in Cosyn's favour was forwarded to the same quarter by certain gentlemen and yeomen of Winchester. The result was that on 24 April, Hilsey, the ex-friar who had just been made Bishop of Rochester, wrote to Dr. Steward informing him that 'Mr. Secretary' had discharged Prior Cosyn, and allowed him 'to use his licence to preach by the authority granted to him by the king, our supreme head next to Christ.'

Cosyn appears to have resigned the priorship, and was succeeded by Richard Chessam, D.D., who was prior when the convent was suppressed in 1538, as already set forth in detail.

Richard Ingworth, the suffragan bishop of Dover, as commissioner for suppressing the friars, forwarded to Thomas Cromwell an inventory of all the goods of the Winchester Dominicans, with their value as appraised by Alderman Burkyn and Master Knight, chosen by the mayor. The inventory, as might be expected of a convent of friars, is a singularly poor and simple one and therefore does them much credit. So few friars' inventories remain that it is well to give it in extenso; it is somewhat surprising to find a pair of organs in a church so sparsely furnished.

The church goods were:—

Viij corporas caasys wythout the corporas, xxd.; iiij surpelys, ijs,; v Coopys for men and ij for chyldren, xijs.; a sute of dune sylke wythout albys, amycis, or stoolys, iijs.; Item, deakyn and subdeakyn of whyet branchyd sylke, without albys, amycis, or stoolys, iijs. iiijd.; a sewte of Whyet chamlet lacking deakyn, xiijs. iiijd.; a syngle vestyment of the same, iiijs.; a complet sute of Whyet bustyan, lacking ij albys, viijs.; iiij syngle vestyments of the same viijs.; a sewte of red sylke xs.; a sewte of blue sylke xvjs.; a sewte of coarse grene xs.; a complete sute of dune sylke without albs, vjs. iiijd.; a syngle vestyment of blue satten, iijs. iiijd,; ix vestyments without albys or stoolys, xs.; ye hangyngs of ye quere, vjd.; a paynted clothe for the Rode, xijd.; a frontelet, xxd.; an albe, xijd.; iij aulter clothys, xiiijd.; ij frontelets, viijd.; ij candelstycks, viijd.; a payre of organs, vs.; an altare (sic) of nedylwerke, xs.

This translates as the following as best as I can make out. Where I cannot translate the word I have left it as written.

"8 Corporas (White linen used to place the bread and wine on) cases without the corporas, 4 surplices, 5 Caps for men and 2 for children, a suit of dun silk without white vestment, amicis (white square of linen worn around the head and neck during mass) or stoles, item, deakin and subdeakin of white branched silk, without albes, amycis or stoles, a suit of White chamlet (camlet-fine white linen made of wool, solk and hair, probably angora) lacking deakyn, a single vestment of the same, a complete suit of white bustian (course cotton fabric), lacking 2 albes, 4 single vestments of the same, a suit of red silk, s suit of blue silk, a suit of coarse green, a complete suit of dun Silk without albes, a single vestment of blue satin 9 vestments without albes of stoles, the hangings of the choir, a painted cloth for the rood, a frontlet, an albe, 3 altar cloths, 2 frontlets, 2 candlesticks A pair of organs, an altare of needlework."

The house contained:—

iij father bedds with iij bolstors ij pillows and j pillow bere and one blankett, xvjs. viijd.; vj payre of scheytts, iijs.; vj Coverletts, xviijd.; a flocke bedde and a mattres, ijs. iiijd.; ye hangyngs and ye tester in ye provyncyalls chamber, iijs.; iij table clothys, j towell, ij tabylls, v chearys, ij joyned stooles, j cupburde, and j oyst' borde, iij formys, j long cheyar, vijs.; a chafyng dysche, vjd.; a possenet, xijd.; a pan and a kettell, xijd; iij platters, iiij pottyngers, j sauser, and iij dysshes, vjs. viijd.; a colender, ij candelstycks, and a sake, xiiijd.; ij dryppyng panys, a fryeng pan, and a gyrdyren, ijs.; iij broochys, ijs.; iij brasse potts, vjs. viijd.; a baasen and an ewer of laten, xvjd.; iiij Cobyrons, iiijs.; a yeryn and hangells to hange on potts, xiiijd.; ij handyryns, vjd."

This translates as the following as best I can make out. Where I cannot translate the word I have left it as written.

"3 feather beds with 3 bolsters 2 pillows and 1 pillow bare and one blanket, 6 pair of sheets, 6 coverlets, a Flock bed and a mattress, the hangings and the tester in the provincials chamber, 3 table cloths, 1 towel, 2 tables, 5 chairs, 2 joined stools, I cupboard, and 1 oyster board, 3 forms, 1 long chair, a chafing dish, a possenet (posnet – pan with long handle and three feet for boiling), a pan and a kettle, 3 platters, 3 pottingers (porringers), 1 saucer and 3 dishes, a colander, 2 candlesticks, and a soak, 2 dripping pans, A frying pan and a gridiron, 1 brochs (spit for roasting), 3 brass pots, a basin and a ewer of laten, 4 cob irons, an urn, and handles to hang on pots, 2 hand irons."

A special chamber assigned for the use of the English provincial points to this convent being considered one of importance in the Order. The total value of church and house goods came to only £9 15s. 2d. To the inventory is appended a note in the suffragan's handwriting to the effect that 'this house with the stuff is in the custody of Master Arthur Roby and a chalice with it. Richard Dovoren.'

The church and the buildings of the cloister, the prior's lodging (20 ft. in length by 16 ft. in breadth), with the churchyard, gardens and all within the precincts, were let by the Crown to Arthur Roby, a fuller of Winchester, for 20s. a year. In 1543, Winchester College, by exchange, became possessed of the site of all the four Winchester friaries.

The archaeology of this site is sparse as it appears the site was demolished comprehensively with just rubble remaining. The stone and good timbers no doubt being reused to help build new houses or repair and expand those already existing. The site was located on Eastgate Street just north of the East Gate. There was, however an excavation in 1989 that revealed some walls near the eastern end of the precinct, probably of the east end of the church. Also found were a cist tomb and a culvert. Other evaluation excavations in 1999 and 2003 close to the city wall at 75-79 Eastgate Street showed extensive demolition rubble which was determined to be from the former friary buildings.

After the dissolution, a survey dated 1543 mentions the church, frater, infirmary, prior's lodgings, a cemetery (located to the south of the church) and gardens.

Priors or Wardens of the Dominicans of Winchester

Matthew, 1242
William de Southampton, elected provincial, 1272, died 1278
Robert de Bromyard, about 1300
Nicholas de Stratton, about 1306
William de Horleye, 1326
Thomas de Lisle

John Payne, 1373
John Derle, 1377, 1387
Nicholas Monk, 1404-26
Walter Alton, 1455
James Cosyn, in the time of Hen. VIII.
Richard Chessam, 1538

The Priory Of St. Swithun, Winchester

The history of this monastery has been already so much dealt with in the Ecclesiastical History of the county that there is comparatively little to add. This monastery, is said to have been founded in honour of Saints Peter and Paul, by Cenwalh, King of Wessex, according to the Anglo-Saxon Chronicle in 643, and according to the Annals of Winchester in 639, and was known after the foundation of New minster or Hyde as the Old Minster.

In the 960's Bishop Ethelwold reformed Old Minster, introducing Benedictine monks in place of the secular canons. It was probably after the rebuilding of the cathedral church by Bishop Aethelwold in 971 that the church and the monastery received the additional dedication in honour of St. Swithun by which it was afterwards known, though the joint dedication to Saints Peter and Paul and St. Swithun lingered on for some time in official documents.

There was apparently no distinction in early times between the lands of the bishop and the lands of the monastery. Grants were made to the church generally, but the lands granted appear to have been under the control of the bishop. About the middle of the tenth century certain lands seem to have been allotted for the maintenance of the monastery, but they remained still under the management of the bishop. At the time of the Domesday Survey the lands allotted for the support of the monks were mostly held by the bishop, those in Hampshire being Chilcombe, Nursling, Chilbolton, Avington, Whitchurch, Freefolk, Witnal in Whitchurch, Hurstbourne Priors, Clere, Crondall, Droxford, Polhampton in Overton, Exton, Alverstoke, Worthy, Wonston, Brainsbury in Barton Stacy, South Stoneham, Millbrook, Hinton

Ampner, Fawley, Etchingswell, Hannington and Hoddington in Upton Gray. The monks themselves held Boarhunt, Wootton St. Laurence, Hayling Island, Brockhampton and Havant. The lands of the bishop and prior formed a great fief for which the bishop owed, at the end of the twelfth century, the service of sixty knights.

There are two chartularies in the British Museum of the priory of St. Swithun, both of which were unknown to the compilers of Dugdale's Monasticon.

The first of these, acquired in 1844 from the dean and chapter of Winchester, contains a large collection of royal and other charters in Anglo-Saxon and Latin, from the reign of Cenwalh of Wessex, 688, to the time of Edward the Confessor, with the addition of a few Norman charters granted by William I, Henry I. and Stephen. It is beautifully written and in good preservation in the original stamped binding; it is supposed to have been compiled between 1130 and 1150.

The other chartulary, acquired in 1873, opens with a brief history of the church to the year 967, followed by a notice of the bishops up to Egbald, in 793. This is followed by charters from the time of Edward the Confessor to 1242. Among the other entries are agreements with the monasteries of Canterbury, Peterborough, Worcester, Gloucester, Reading, Tewkesbury, Chertsey, Burton, Ely, Abingdon, St. Albans, St. Pancras at Lewes, Glastonbury, Durham, Merton, Malmesbury, Bury St. Edmunds, Westminster, Wherwell, Romsey, Bec (Normandy) and Battle, as to mutual masses for the dead; a list of plate and vestments, the gifts of Bishop Henry de Blois; notices of the deaths and benefactions of Bishop William de Raleigh (1243) and Bishop John of Exeter (1262); copies of charters and agreements between priors and bishops, and as to pensions or oblations of parochial clergy from 1284 to 1334; together with the comuetudines elemosine and other customs of the church. The chartulary contains eighty-three folios, and was compiled in the thirteenth century, save that there are a few fifteenth century entries towards the end.

The prior furnished Thomas Cromwell, on his appointment as general visitor, with a succinct account of the early history of their house from the year 604, giving what they termed the annals of their first, second, third and fourth foundations. There is a copy of this in the Harley manuscripts. Held by the British Library, the Harleian collection comprises more than 7,000 manuscripts, 14,000 charters and 500 rolls. Most are in European languages, including a sizeable number in Greek; the library also includes items in Hebrew and oriental languages.

In September, 1243, the monks of St. Swithun obtained papal sanction to wear caps (pilleis) in quire on account of the cold, provided that due reverence was shown at the gospel and the elevation. In the same month pope Innocent IV issued his mandate to the priors of Rochester and of Holy Trinity, London, in a matter affecting this priory. The convent of Winchester had complained that, on the voidance of the priory (1239), Andrew, a monk, by secular force and by the assistance of the archdeacons of Winchester and Surrey, had obtruded himself into the office of prior.

Andrew was therefore excommunicated by the Archbishop of Canterbury; but of this he took no heed, and introducing an armed band into the cloister by night, ill-used, bound and imprisoned Richard de Triveri and many other monks. Further, at his instance, the archdeacon of Winchester issued sentences of excommunication and suspension against many members of the convent. The pope ordered the two priors to go to Winchester, to relax provisionally the archdeacon's sentences, and if, on examination, the facts justified it, to provide a prior by canonical election. At the same date a papal faculty was forwarded to the sub-prior and convent of Winchester to use their privileges, although they had not done so for a long time on account of their ignorance of the law, the disturbance of the realm, and the change of prelates of the see. This was accompanied by a general licence to the priory to administer their property, wherein is recited the particulars of their manors, advowsons, pensions and other rights.

The monks paid dearly for yielding to the pressure exercised by the Crown in the matter of the election of Aymer to the bishopric. Soon after his election Aymer treated them with the utmost indignity and violence, driving the prior and his obedientiaries from the house. In 1254 Prior William de Andrew visited Rome to lay his grievances before the papal court. Pope Innocent IV treated him with every consideration, and granted to him and his successors the use of mitre, ring, tunicle, dalmatic, gloves and sandals; the right of blessing chalices, altar palls and other church ornaments; the giving of the first tonsure; the conferring of the minor orders of doorkeeper and reader; and the giving of solemn benediction in divine offices and at table.

The disturbed state of the unfortunate monastery at this period of its history is shown by a patent issued by Henry III in July, 1255. It took the shape of a precept to the abbots and priors throughout England, inhibiting them from receiving into their monasteries and houses any of the monks of Winchester, very many of whom of their own will and pleasure wander all over England in contempt and despite of monastic religion, and to the peril of their own souls, unless by letters of permission from the elect of Winchester or the prior of the same place.

It was not until 1256 that this quarrel between bishop and prior was temporarily settled. The right of the monks to elect their own prior was formally conceded in 1258, but this was again disputed in 1266, and once more settled in their favour in 1273.

On 4 May, 1264, the citizens of Winchester rose against the monks and burnt the priory gateway, the gate called Kingsgate, the upper part of the church (ecclesia) of St. Swithun, and all the houses near the wall that belonged to the convent. The annal writers do not mention any cause for this popular tumult, which was sufficiently severe to cause the death of several of the prior's servants.

Considerable disputes again arose between the Bishop of Winchester and the prior of St. Swithun's at the beginning of the rule of Bishop Pontoise, as to the appointment of the obedientiaries or officials of the monastery. In October, 1282, the bishop appointed Ralph Chaunterel, one of his attendants, to the important office of kitchener to the priory, stating in his register that it was on account of his faithful service to him. In the following year the bishop collated John de Nortwold to the still more important office of cellarer; this appointment is entered in his register among other collations and institutions to benefices.

This last nomination gave rise to vigorous remonstrance on the part of the prior and convent. Eventually in July, 1284, the bishop covenanted to yield to the prior the liberty of appointing and removing obedientiaries and secular servants; but the priory did not obtain this covenant in their favour without making a substantial concession. On the same day and year that this episcopal ordinance was issued the prior and convent conceded to the bishop the very valuable manors of Droxford, Alverstoke and Havant. As the Crown had on several occasions appointed obedientiaries and sergeants for the monastery during the vacancy of the see, it was thought well to obtain royal sanction for this episcopal ordinance. Consequently Edward I., in September, 1284, granted letters patent confirming the episcopal covenant, and also granting to the prior the power of appointing to the sergeanties or other secular offices pertaining to the house. At the same time the chapter was granted the custody of the priory during voidance.

About ten days after the sealing of the covenant between the bishop and priory, through the resignation of William de Basing, there was a vacancy in the office of prior, and the bishop, with the unanimous assent of his brethren, put the custody of the house into the hands of Nicholas de Merewell (Marwell?), the subprior. On the same day (13 July) the bishop issued a letter to the retiring prior and the obedientiaries giving them absolution after certain scandals, the nature of which is not stated. On 18 July the sub-prior and chapter asked leave of the bishop to elect a new prior; in the bishop's letter of sanction he referred to the resignation of Prior William, stating that it was not caused through any crime or conscious fault, but for the sake of humility and true religion.

On 25 August, 1284, the bishop gave his assent to the election of William de Basing as prior, and issued the usual injunction to the sub-prior and convent to yield him due obedience. From this it would appear that the ex-prior was, with episcopal assent, re-elected.

Bishop John of Pontoise was probably anxious to see if the re-election was satisfactory, for on 14 September he issued notice of a personal visitation of the cathedral priory to be held at the ensuing Michaelmas. As no injunctions were issued consequent on this visitation it may be assumed that everything was found to be satisfactory.

By 1291 the possessions of the prior seem to have been definitely separated from those of the bishop, and the estates of the former had considerably increased. The total yearly value was £701 0s. 7d. At the same time it will be noticed that as late as 1346 the bishop owed the service of five knights' fees for his own land and also for all the lands of the prior. From the aid for making Edward the Black Prince a knight in this year we find that the prior of St. Swithun's held with John Frilende half a knight's fee in ' Nywenton '; he held also with two others half a fee in Stoke in St. Mary Bourne (Crokerestok), and half a fee in Long Sutton.

On the death of Prior William in May, 1295, leave to elect was applied for and granted by the bishop. The monks on this occasion elected by way of 'compromise.' The chapter appointed William de Hoo, Adam de Hyde, Roger de Entingham, Henry Bacun, Henry de Merwell, Nicholas de Tarente and William Wallup to act as electors. Their choice eventually fell upon Henry de Merweli alias Woodlock, and the bishop's assent was given on 7 June. The particulars as to this election are set forth in the episcopal register with much detail.

On 13 June, 1305, Bishop Henry granted leave to fill up the vacancy in the priory, caused by his own elevation to the episcopate, and gave the custody during the vacancy to William de Somborne, John de Donketon and Ralph de Canne. On 31 July entry was made in the episcopal register of the process of election, and a week later the bishop's consent to the appointment of Nicholas de Tarente was signified, and he was duly installed. The bishop visited the priory in 1308, and apparently found nothing to correct.

In 1297 mandate was issued by the Crown to the justice of the forest to permit the prior to grant and make stable-stands, according to the term of the king's charter to him and his successors, in the demesne lands and woods where they had chases in Hampshire, and to carry away venison, and to keep their dogs not expeditated, but on condition that they set or stretched no nets for taking such venison. John de Ford, monk of St. Swithun's, received a royal pardon in June, 1344, for taking a doe and a sorel in the New Forest and carrying them away. At the same time Prior Alexander was pardoned for receiving the said doe and sorel.

The various acta relative to the election of Richard de Eneford as prior are briefly cited in Henry de Woodlock's register under the date of 8 September, 1309.

An important visitation of the priory of St. Swithun's was held by the bishop in 1315, which resulted in a considerable number of injunctions. The greater part of these are of the usual character, and partake more of enjoining a careful observance of the rule than of dealing with any particular delinquency. Such were orders to attend all the offices, night and day; frequent celebrating by the monks in priest's orders; silence at the appointed time and places; never to break bounds without leave; to speak to no women, religious or secular, save in public; to wear nought save the statutory dress; and juniors to respect seniors. Others related to the due keeping of the cloister gate, to the custody of the seal, and to the annual rendering of accounts by obedientiaries and bailiffs. Two or three are less usual, and probably refer to specific faults, such as directions against selling surplus food, and that parents or relatives visiting the inmates were to be invited to contribute according to their means. One order has a decidedly local touch, by which all the monks, save the sacrist and his servants, are forbidden to go out of the monastery by the gate called ' Redebreck '. The bishop had the advantage in this visitation of full personal knowledge of the house during the ten years that he was prior.

In the second year of Bishop Stratford's rule (1325), a complete list of the monks of St. Swithun was drawn up. It begins with Prior Richard;

the second name, presumably the sub-prior, is Adam de Hyde, and then follow the names of sixty-two other monks.

Bishop Stratford held two visitations of St. Swithun's during the ten years that he administered the see. In the last case penalties were imposed and then taken off. The priory was visited in February, 1410-1, by John Cattyk, chancellor of the diocese. He visited as the commissary of the diocesan, Bishop Henry Beaufort stating that he was not able personally to visit owing to the pressure of other arduous affairs.

The earlier episcopal registers are for the most part somewhat sparing in their reference to the work and administration of the cathedral priory, but the entries are frequent in William of Wykeham's days.

The rectory of the church of Littleton was appropriated to the office of guest-master of the priory in the year 1171. In March, 1373, Bishop William of Wykeham licensed John Hyde, the monk guest-master, to hear confessions and to administer the Eucharist at Littleton during Lent and at Easter, for the depression of the times prevented the parishioners employing a parochial chaplain to assist the vicar. The licence was to expire at the end of the Easter octave. This temporary and useful licence was renewed to the guest-master year by year up to 1379.

Hugh Basing was prior when Wykeham was elected bishop. On his death in 1384 Dr. Robert Rudborne succeeded, and he was followed in 1394 by Dr. Thomas Neville. The friction between bishops and priors is illustrated by the action that took place during Wykeham's episcopate with regard to a comparatively trifling but very interesting custom dating back to time immemorial. According to this ancient custom whenever the diocesan visited Wolvesey, or any other residence in Winchester, the domicellus of the priory presented him with eight loaves of fine wheat flour and four gallons of wine, saying at the same time these words in French: *"Moumeigneur, Seint Pere et Seint Paule vous envoient."* Prior Hugh set the example of reducing the offering to a single loaf and one gallon of wine, and his example was followed by

Prior Rudborne and by Prior Neville for the first four years of his office. But in 1398, other disputes having arisen, a covenant was made between Wykeham and Neville for the resumption of the full customary offering of bread and wine, and that the ancient words should be said in French, Latin or English. At the same time it was agreed that disputes between the tenants of their respective estates should be tried in the bishop's or prior's court and not in those of the king; that the priory should maintain the bridge over the Lockburn in College Street, and halve the expense with bishop of the bridge over the river; and that the priory should abstain from feeding sheep or taking rabbits in the episcopal chase and warren at Morestead. In June, 1373, Wykeham visited the priory and was apparently content with its condition, as no injunctions were entered.

Another visitation of the cathedral priory was arranged by the bishop to be held in the autumn of 1386, but in November a mandate was issued postponing it, in consequence of urgent business, to 10 February. On 6 February, 1386-7, Wykeham addressed a letter to the prior and convent on the serious reduction in their numbers, and two days later he directed his official and another to conduct the visitation on 10 February. It was at this time that the bishop issued a code of directions or revised rule for the guidance of the monks, providing in various ways against laxity. The number of the monks was at that time reduced to forty-six. It still stood at that figure during a third visitation, 1393, and though Wykeham again specially insisted on the raising of their numbers, the roll had fallen to forty-two at the time of his death.

Much of the administration of the priory can be learnt from some of the old account rolls that still survive. A fourteenth-century roll in the possession of the dean and chapter contains an interesting account of the obligations of the officers of the priory in connection with the frater. *"The prior was bound to provide the frater with bread, beer, wine, salt, cheese and butter; also with the necessary rush-woven mats and with straw litter for the floor. Cheese was to be served daily at dinner and supper from Easter Day to Quinquagesima Sunday, and butter on Wednesdays and Saturdays from 1 May to 14 September. New mats were to be furnished on the vigil of All Saints, and fresh straw seven times a year. The chamberlain provided a new cloth for the high table every Palm Sunday, and canvas cloths for the other tables as often as necessary; he had also to find old cloths for cleansing the silver and other vessels. The sacrist had to send the fraterer fifteen wax candles on the vigil of All Saints, to be renewed as often as needful down to Maundy Thursday. The precentor. and his fellows, who on Sunday and other feasts at 12 o'clock (after nones) have said the Placebo, were to have a 'punchard' of good beer. The almoner was to give the fraterer a clapper (signum) on Maundy Thursday. The kitchener was to receive his food daily with the under-cooks, but was to sit at the high table and have a punchard. The gardener was to provide apples on Mondays, Wednesdays and Fridays in Advent and Lent; the sub-prior, third prior and fourth prior, the fraterer and other officers were to have ten apples each; if the prior was present he was to have fifteen. The same was to be done on St. James' Day, when there was the blessing of apples. At the east end of the frater, between the windows, stood a celebrated old cross or crucifix, from which, according to tradition, a voice proceeded, deciding the controversy between St. Dunstan and the ejected secular canons. The guardian of the altar of Our Lady and the keeper of the cloister garth had to provide tapers to burn before this cross on certain high days, and the fraterer to provide seven branches to burn in the like place daily during the second collation. The custom of carrying round the ancient cup of St. Athelwold to be kissed by all on his festival has been already described. The cellarer had his meals with the community; it was his duty to provide meat and drink and food of every kind, to produce and keep in repair all the necessary vessels for the cellar, kitchen and frater, to attend to the lighting of the chandelier and of the three flat lamps that hung before the cross. A curious entry further records that he was to have the care of all the animals acquired by different brethren. Pet animals were frequently found in religious houses: occasionally visitors ordered their expulsion, particularly squirrels and birds in cages, from nunneries. The curtarian looked after the due allowance of bread, and the corrodies or due provision for bishops, kings and other visitors. It was the porter's duty to clean out the frater against Easter, and to make the fire on the hearth in snowy weather".*

The daily life of these Benedictine monks can be traced from point to point in the large number of Obedientiary Rolls of the different officials of the house that still survive of the fourteenth, fifteenth and sixteenth centuries. The obedientiaries were monks told off to fulfil certain duties, and to superintend particular parts of the administration of the convent and its property. Their duty at St. Swithun's was essentially connected with the exercise of hospitality; their priory lay in a chief city on one of the most important highways in England, and it was their well sustained boast to keep open house for all comers. In this and in other respects the monks of the cathedral priory of the diocese maintained on the whole an excellent character. The ideal number of monks at which all the large Benedictine houses was supposed to aim was seventy; but this was seldom attained. In 1325, as has been stated, the roll reached to sixty-four; but the priory never recovered from the staggering blow of the Black Death. The numbers, even under the stirring episcopate of Bishop Wykeham, did not exceed forty-six, and at his death were only forty-two. Only once did they subsequently rise, and that by a single figure, the total in 1533 being forty-three. The Obedientiary Rolls show that the lowest level was in 1495-6, when the numbers were only twenty-nine.

Dean Kitchin, in his introduction to the Obedientiary Rolls, makes a helpful division of the monastic officials of St. Swithun's into four groups, a division which applies broadly speaking not only to other Benedictine houses, but to most of the other religious orders:—

(a) Round the Prior (the most dignified personage, the bishop acting as abbot) were grouped the Subprior, the third Prior, and the fourth Prior, who all had definite claustral duties to fulfil. This group was responsible for the general order of the house. With these may be associated the land Steward, who was not a monk, and who is usually described as the prior's steward.

(b) The second group was attached to the church, and included the Sacrist and Subsacrist who had charge of all material things pertaining to the services; the Chanter and Subchanter, who were responsible for the actual conduct of divine worship; the Anniversarian, who had charge of the obit days of benefactors;

and the Warden of the Works, who looked after all repairs of the church and other buildings.

(c) The internal officers of the house were the Receiver, to whom were paid the rents of the several estates; the Hordarian, who had charge of the material resources of the convent supplying the frater, etc., and also having charge of estates and income specially assigned for such purposes; the Refectorian who received all the eatables, passing them on to the Kitchener; the Chamberlain, who had charge of the furniture; the Cellarer who looked after the beer and wine and took charge of all the outbuildings and stables; the Almoner who distributed to the poor in kind and money; and the infirmarer, or physician monk in charge of the infirmary.

(d) The fourth was a little group of officers dealing with external affairs, as the Outer and Inner Porters, and the Guest-master.
The extant Obedientiary Rolls of St. Swithun's are most numerous in connection with the office of hordarian, of which there are fifteen, and of the almoner, of which there are thirty-two. The Diet Roll for 1492 describes precisely how the Winchester monks fed at their two meals, apart from beer and vegetables, which are not entered. On an ordinary day, such as the Monday before Christmas, they had on the table a dish of marrow and grated bread, eggs, venison, beef, mutton and calves' feet. On Christmas Day they had in addition onion broth, the total cost being 10s. 9d. against 8s. 4d. of the previous Monday. On a day of strict fast, such as Friday in Passion week, they had salt fish, figs and raisins, and rice. Another interesting item is that the monk gardener of St. Swithun's was bound to provide flowers to deck the church at certain festivals, as well as to find the apples for Advent and Lent consumption.

Bishop Fox visited St. Swithun's on 26 August, 1521, and subsequently (1 February, 1521-2) issued a variety of injunctions that tell of some disorder. The injunctions open with blaming the chanter and subchanter for lack of quire books, and that those in use were torn (rupta) and out of repair. The most interesting rebuke to the monks was that they neglected to choose scholars to send to the University of Oxford in accordance with the Benedictine constitutions.

The election of Henry Brook as prior in the time of Bishop Fox is set forth with great circumstance in his registers. Application for licence to elect was made in December, 1524, but the new prior was not installed until 7 March, 1524-5.

Dr. Hede, commissary of the prior of Canterbury, during the vacancy of the Sees of both Canterbury and Winchester, visited St. Swithun's on 27 February, 1500.

In addition to Thomas Silkstede, the prior, the following office holders were examined at the visitation: Thomas Manhouse, sub-prior; John Dorsett, third prior; John Pury, gardener; Richard Aunstell, sacrist; Philip Yong, almoner; Thomas Cyan, hordarian; John Stonkton, master of the works; Walter Hyll, firmarius; John Beste, hostilar; John Cerne, deposttarius; John Wodesun, warden of Our Lady; Peter Marlow, chanter; Arnold Gylbert, chamberlain; John Westbury, curtarian; Henry Broke, fourth prior; and Tympany Alt, depositarius. Twelve others were also examined, giving a total of twenty-nine who appeared before the visitor. Of these three were deacons, one a sub-deacon, and one an acolyte. Two are simply entered as professed of the order of St. Benedict, and were novices: Thomas Manydon, aged 16, who had been three weeks in the monastery, and Fulk Hampton, 18, who had been there for a like period; neither of them had as yet received the first tonsure. The evidence was wholly in favour of the order and administration of the house. The statutory number of the monks was at that time reduced to forty, and there were then only thirty-five, but the treasurer reminded the visitor that there had been five recent deaths. At the close of the evidence Dr. Hede's only injunction was as to the speedy filling up of the full number of the monks. The visitor called upon the prior to take an oath of canonical obedience to the prior and convent of Canterbury during the vacancy of the see, and to the Archbishop of Canterbury when the see was filled. Prior Silkestede however declined, unless the prior of Canterbury took an oath to observe the rights of the cathedral church in the same way as the Bishop of Winchester did at the time of his consecration. The question was adjourned till the following day, when Silkestede submitted.

The story of the end of St. Swithun's as a monastery, and the desolation effected in the church in September, 1538, is a common tale across the country at this time.

At the time of the dissolution the monastery held the manors of Nursling, Millbrook Morecourt, Hursley, 'Oxenbridge,' Avington, Exton, 'Hadington,' Bransbury, Up Somborne, ' Henton, Wymanston,' the city of Winchester and the soke, and lands and rents in Dean and Lovington in Hampshire; and the manors of 'Hynxton,' Overton with the rectory, Alton with the rectory, Stocketon, Patney, West wood ' Langfischedide' next Endford, and Shipton Bellinger in Wiltshire; and the manor of Bleadon in Somersetshire, as well as pensions from divers churches.

The steps by which the ancient Benedictine house of St. Swithun was turned into a dean and chapter in 1539-42 is well documented but was not without its issues as there was no precedent. A whole series of documents touching this change, eleven in number, are extant at Winchester, and have been printed and edited by Dean Kitchin. The first letters patent formally establishing the new body are dated 28 March, 1542.

On 1 May, 1542, the newly-formed dean and chapter were endowed with the following manors and lands, most of which had previously belonged to the prior and convent, viz. Avington, Berthon Priors, Bransbury, Chilbolton, Crondall, Exton, Haddington, Hanton, 'Littleton,' Manydown, Millbrook, Moorecourt, Nursling, Silkstead, Sutton, Upsomborne, West Meon, Whitchurch and 'Wonsington' in Hampshire; and Alton, Ham, Hinton 'Langefysshehre 'near Endford, Overton, Patney, Shipton Bellinger, Stockton, Westwood, 'Winnaston' and Wroughton in Wiltshire, and Bleadon in Somerset.

The possessions of the dean and chapter in 1682 consisted of the Hampshire manors of Barton and Newhouse, Sparsholt and Wyke,

Compton, Sparkford and 'Fulflood,' Chilcombe and Morstead, 'Winnall,' Ovington and 'Brixden,' Crondall, Sutton, Manydown, 'Boghurst,' Hannington, Whitchurch, Freefolk, Charlcott, 'Wonsington,' Bransbury, Chilbolton, Littleton, Up Somborne, 'Thurmonds,' Silkstead, Exton, Hinton Ampner, Shipton, Morecourt and Oxenbridge, Lovington, the city of Winchester, office of woodward and the liberty of the fair of St. Mary Magdalene; in the county of Wilts the manor of Hinton, Ham, 'Bechinstoke,' Botwell and Longstreet, Wroughton, Little Alton, Westwood, 'Elmestubb' and Eversley, and a large number of churches in both counties.

The manors of inheritance, which belonged to the dean and chapter and were handed over to the ecclesiastical commissioners in 1861, were Crondall with Sutton, Warblington, and Hinton Ampner.

Priors of St. Swithun Of Winchester
Brithnoth, about 970, made abbot of Ely
Brithwold, about 1006, became Bishop of Winchester
Elfric Puttoc, 1023, made Archbishop of York
Wulfsig, died 1065
Simon or Simeon, 1065-82, brother to Bishop Walkelyn, made abbot of Ely
Godfrey, 1082-1107.
Geoffrey, 1107-11. He was deposed Geoffrey II, 1111-4, made abbot of Burton, Staffordshire
Eustace, 1114-20
Hugh, 1120
Geoffrey III., died in 1126
Ingulph, made abbot of Abingdon in 1130
Robert, 1130-6, made Bishop of Bath and Wells
Robert II., 1173, made abbot of Glastonbury
Walter, 1171-5, made abbot of Westminster
John, died 1187
Robert III., surnamed Fitzhenry, made abbot of Burton Roger, 1214
Walter IL, died 1239
Andrew, 1239
Walter III., 1243, resigned in 1247

John de Cauz, 1247-9, in latter year made abbot of Peterborough

William Taunton, 1249-56, made abbot of Middleton in Dorsetshire, and afterwards elected Bishop of Winchester, but the election was invalidated

Andrew of London, 1258-61, resigned Ralph Russel, 1261-5

Valentine, 1265-76, deprived John de Dureville, 1276 -8

Adam de Farnham, 1279, excommunicated for disobedience July, 1282, and absolved in the following month

William de Basynge, 1282, resigned in 1284, but was re-elected the same year; finally resigned in 1295

Henry Wodelock, alias Mereville, 12951305, made Bishop of Winchester

Nicholas de Tarente, 1305-9

Richard de Enford, 1309, 1326

Alexander Heriard, 1327, died 1349

John Merlaw, 1349-56

Hugh Basyng, 1356-84

Robert Rudborne, 1384-95

Thomas Nevil, 1395

Thomas Shyrebourn

William Aulton, died 1450

Richard Marlborough, 1450-7

Robert Westgate, 1457-70

Thomas Hinton, 1470-98

Thomas Silkested, 1498-1524

Henry Brook, 1524-35

William Basyng, alias Kingsmill, 1535-9

Deans Of Winchester Cathedral

William Kingsmill, D.D., 1541-8

Sir John Mason, knt. (layman), 1549-53

Edmund Steward, LL.D., 1554-9

John Warner, M.D., 1559-64

Francis Newton, D.D., 1565-72

John Watson, M.D., 1573-80 (Bishop of Winchester, 1580)

Lawrence Humphrey, D.D., 1580-89

Martin Heton, D.D., 1589-99. (Bishop of Ely, 1599)
George Abbot, D.D., 1599-1600-9. (Bishop of Lichfield and Coventry, 1609; London, 1610; Archbishop of Canterbury, 1611)
Thomas Morton, D.D., 1610-16. (Bishop of Chester, 1616)
John Young, D.D., 1616—dispossessed by the Commonwealth
Alexander Hyde, LL.D., 1660-5. (Bishop of Salisbury, 1665)
William Clark, D.D., 1666-79
Richard Meggott, D.D., 1679-92
John Wickart, D.D., 1693-1721
William Trimnell, D.D., 1722-9
Charles Naylor, LL.D., 1729-39
Zachary Pearce, D.D., 1739-48. (Bishop of Bangor, 1748)
Thomas Cheyney, D.D., 1748-60
Jonathan Shipley, D.D., 1760-9. (Bishop of Llandaff, St. Asaph, 1769)
Newton Ogle, D.D., 1769-1804
Robert Holmes, 1804-5
Thomas Rennell, D.D., 1805-40
Thomas Gamier, D.C.L., 1840-1871
John Bramston, D.D., 1872-83
George William Kitchin, D.D. 1873-1895
William Richard Wood Stephens, D.D., 1895-1902

New Minster, Or The Abbey Of Hyde

The extensive abbey at Hyde to the north of Winchester city centre no longer exists but over recent years, through community archaeological digs, the abbey buildings are starting to re-emerge, only in bits and pieces. Victorian terraced houses now site on the site of the former abbey and it is in the gardens of these houses that significant finds have been uncovered that can add to the story of the site.

This includes a reappraisal of the layout of the abbey buildings as walls found during these archaeological digs do not appear where they were expected to be using a standard abbey layout of the time. Variation in layout could be down to various factors like geography, geology, inheriting an established site with buildings in situ. More digs are due to be carried out over the coming years and these may answer some of these questions.

The abbey of the Holy Trinity, the Blessed Virgin Mary, and St. Peter of the New Minster in Winchester was founded in 901 by Edward the Elder in accordance with the wishes of his father King Alfred. It would appear that towards the close of the ninth century Alfred, being anxious to promote the better education of the children of his nobles, summoned Grimbald, a learned priest and monk of St. Bertin at St. Omer in Flanders to assist him in this work. Grimbald arrived in 893, but it was not till the last year of his reign that Alfred told him of his intention to build a new monastery at his royal borough of Winchester. The king only lived long enough to purchase the site for the monastery in the open churchyard immediately to the north of the cathedral or the Old Minster from Bishop Denewulph and the canons of the Old Minster and others. It was left to Edward the Elder to carry out his father's intention to build the monastery and to place Grimbald there as the first Abbot.

The Church was consecrated in 903 and in the same year Edward endowed the monastery with considerable possessions, including the land of Micheldever and lands of Stratton, 'Burcote,' Popham, Woodmancote, Candover, Cranborne, Drayton juxta Nunneton, 'Swarraton, Northingtone, Norton juxta Selborne, 'Slastede,' Tatchbury, Abbots Anne, 'Colengaburna, 'Ceoseldene' and Durley. At this time also the church was enriched with the relics of St. Judoc or Josse the confessor, which were brought there by certain monks of Ponthieu who fled to England from Danish raiders.

Shortly after the dedication of the church the remains of Alfred were carried in solemn procession to the New Minster from their temporary resting-place in the church of St. Swithun or the Old Minster in Winchester and buried on the right side of the altar. In the same tomb were also interred Edward's mother, Queen Ealhswith, foundress of Nunnaminster, and afterwards the bodies of Edward and his two sons, Ethelward and Elfward, were buried in a tomb adjoining that of his parents. At a later date the New Minster became the burial place for several members of the Saxon royal house.

The church was served by secular canons, who, as it is said by the later chroniclers that had no sympathy with the seculars and married priests, permitted great laxity of discipline and were the cause of scandal. About 963 Aethelwold, Bishop of Winchester, with the approval of King Edgar and St. Dunstan, as a part of his scheme for monastic reform in his diocese, insisted upon the adoption of the Benedictine rule by the inmates of New Minster under pain of expulsion, and King Edgar supplied a series of laws to be used by the monastery. The majority of the house refused to accept the new rules and were driven from the monastery, their places being taken by regular monks from Abingdon, over whom Ethelgar was placed as abbot. Ethelgar, like most of the Church reformers of this date, was a man of distinct individuality; he had received his monastic training under Ethelwold at Abingdon and upon his appointment to New Minster he took in hand the reform of the monastery with the zeal copied from his late master. Not only did he look to the rule of the house, but he carried out various works on the buildings including the erection of a tower, said to be of great height and beauty, and a richly carved ceiling. He became Bishop of Selsey in 980 and succeeded St. Dunstan as Archbishop of Canterbury in 988.

King Cnut was a great benefactor to the Minster, not only in lands but by the gift of the golden cross richly adorned with precious stones with two great images of gold and silver and sundry relics of saints. Among other benefactions received by the monastery at about this time was the gift in 1041 by Queen Emma, widow of Cnut, of the head of St. Valentine, which was cherished as one of the most valuable possessions of the house.

Alwyn, brother of Earl Godwin, became abbot in 1064. During his abbacy a disastrous fire destroyed a considerable part of the domestic buildings of the Minster on St. George's Day, 1066. This abbot naturally took the part of his nephew Harold in resisting the Norman invasion, and according to the register of the monastery he was slain in battle on the field of Hastings. Mr. Round has already dealt with the question of the supposed active part that the monks of New Minster took at the battle of Hastings, and has shown from the Domesday

Survey how considerable are the exaggerations usually current with regard to the consequent confiscations of the Conqueror. At the time of the Survey the Abbey held in Hampshire, Brown Candover, Woodmancote, Fullerton in Wherwell, Leckford, Micheldever, Cranbourne, Drayton in Barton Stacey, West Stratton, East Popham, Abbot's Worthy, Alton, Worting, Bighton, Bedhampton, Lomer in Corhampton, Warnford, Lickpit in Basing, North Stoneham, Kingsclere, Tatchbury in Eling, Abbots Anne, and Laverstoke.

Not long after the Conquest evil days fell upon the abbey. On the death of Rewalan the Red King made his 'infamous chancellor,' Ralph Flambard, abbot. By an openly simoniacal arrangement between the abbot-chancellor and the king, Herbert Losinga, Bishop of Norwich, bought the New Minster for his father, Robert Losinga, who was appointed abbot in 1091. On the death of Abbot Robert in 1093, the unhappy abbey again fell into the unscrupulous hands of Ralph Flambard. Relief however came to this scandal with the accession of Henry Beauclerk in 1100, when Hugh, a monk of St. Swithun's, was appointed abbot.

The will of the next abbot, Geoffrey, was one of singular moment to the abbey; the register styles him "Fundator Hide (Hyde)". In 1109 the monks were enabled to leave their crowded site, the cause of many a serious inconvenience, and move to commodious quarters on the north side of Winchester, just beyond the city walls, known as Hyde Mead. Henceforth this important Benedictine house was known as Hyde Abbey. The old site was surrendered into the king's hands, and was shortly afterwards restored to the cathedral church of St. Swithun. To the monks of Hyde the king granted another charter, whereby, amongst other regulations, it was arranged that a joint procession of the monks of St. Swithun and Hyde was to be made year by year. Their new home was speedily ready for occupation, and in 1110 the monks of New Minster carried with them to the Abbey of Hyde, in solemn procession, their sacred relics, the great gold cross of Cnut's benefaction, together with the illustrious remains of Alfred, his queen and his son. Henry I. made several grants to the abbey, among them the churches of Kingsclere and Alton and 5 hides in Alton which William I. had given in exchange for land in the city of Winchester. He also confirmed to them the right of soc and sac, thol and theam and other liberties.

To Geoffrey succeeded Osbert in 1124. The length of his rule is somewhat uncertain, but it probably ended in 1135. The new abbey, however, only lasted for thirty years, for when the city was fired in 1141, in the midst of the fierce civil war between the adherents of Maud and Stephen, the Abbey of Hyde perished in the conflagration. Then for several years there was continuous strife between the monks of Hyde and the high born and imperious Bishop Henry de Blois. By him, say the Hyde annal writers, *"was the great cross of Cnut burnt"*, alluding to its loss in the great fire, when the bishop directed fireballs to be thrown from his castle of Wolvesey into that quarter of the city adjoining the abbey.

In 1142 Hugh de Lens succeeded as abbot after a vacancy of six years. There was much internal dissension at this time, and in 1149 a large deputation of the monks proceeded to Rome to complain of their abbot, as well as to renew their charges against their diocesan. Hugh was removed, and for two years the abbey was again vacant, whilst Bishop Henry endeavoured to persuade the Pope to convert his ancient see to an archiepiscopate, and to make Hyde Abbey the centre of one of his suffragan bishoprics. The scheme however failed, and Selid was elected abbot in 1151. In the seventeenth year of his abbacy, the continuous suits against the bishop were at last decided in favour of Hyde, and amongst other acts of restitution the bishop presented to the abbey as skilful a reproduction of Cnut's golden cross as the art of the day could furnish. After its destruction by fire some parts of the abbey were rebuilt, but the work was very gradual. The thorough reconstruction of the great church was not even begun until 1182.

Selid died in 1171, the same year as Bishop Henry, when there was again a vacancy for about five years. In 1177 Thomas, the Prior of Montacute, a Cluniac house in Somerset, became abbot; he resigned his office in 1181. He was succeeded by John Suthill, during whose vigorous rule of nearly forty-two years the abbey prospered and enjoyed much internal peace. In 1185 this abbot proceeded to Rome to bring back the pall for Baldwin, Archbishop-elect of Canterbury. In 1208 John restored the temporalities which had been taken into his hands by reason of the interdict. The abbot at this time owed the service of twenty knights to the Crown for his lands.

The year after Suthill's appointment (1182) the annal writers tell of a miraculous appearance of St. Barnabas at an altar dedicated to his honour, and it was this incident that gave an impetus to the church restoration. There were various other remarkable manifestations at this altar, which caused the faithful to flock to the abbey, and the saint became the object of a special cult at Hyde. Henceforth the monks were frequently described as monks of St. Barnabas.

In 1267 there was a serious affray in the abbey between the servants of the abbot and those of the pope's legate, Otho, who had come to Hyde to keep the festival of Christmas with a great retinue, and who observed the feast with too much conviviality.

A curious faculty, which throws some light upon the condition of monastic life in the thirteenth century, was granted by Pope Nicholas IV. in 1288 to this abbey, by which permission was granted to the monks to wear caps of sheep or lamb skin at the divine offices and processions, the cold in those parts, it was said, having caused paralysis and other diseases to some of the monks.

In 1302 royal licence was obtained for the appropriation (in accordance with a patent of 1292) of the church of Micheldever and its chapels, of the annual value of £70, to which the bishop had already assented, on condition that the revenue should be applied to the use of guests and of the poor and infirm persons who flocked to the abbey. Various impediments arose to this appropriation, but at last it was confirmed by Pope Clement V. in 1309, and papal mandates to that effect were sent to the Archdeacon of Winchester and to the Chapter of Salisbury; in the same year there was the like papal confirmation of the appropriation of the church of Alton.

There were several visitations of the monastery during the first half the fourteenth century, and in 1312 Bishop Woodlock had occasion to inhibit the convent from using the common seal for any alienation. Again in 1318 Bishop Sandaie addressed a stern letter to the abbot bidding him check the careless monks who neglected meditation, and their claustral duties, and complaining of the lukewarmness of his rule. Odiham's rule was but brief. On 21 May, 1319, the abbot was seriously ill, and the monks sent their steward to the king to try and arrange for the custody of the temporalities, during the expected vacancy. The abbot however died on June 5 before the matter could be arranged, so that it was not until June 10 that the monks received the agreement, whereby it was arranged that the convent might retain the custody on payment of 200 marks to the Crown, provided the vacancy did not exceed two months.

Walter de Fifield, a monk of the house, had the temporalities restored to him as abbot (the agreement of June 10 being held to be void) on August 1. Between this abbot and his convent there were many disputes, the chief contention of the prior and brethren being that he was wrongfully increasing the separate abbatial revenue at the expense of the house at large. The matter came frequently before Bishop Stratford, with the result that the abbot was virtually acquitted. The bishop made a formal visitation of the abbey in February, 1325, and issued as the result an elaborate series of decrees, which were in the main of the usual character. The attendance of all at the night and day offices was enjoined; brothers in priest's orders were to celebrate daily; close custody was to be kept of the doors; the disturbance caused by boys chattering on the south side of the infirmary was to be stopped; the access of men and women into the church and cloister at inordinate hours and times was to cease; no brother was to frequent the nunneries of Winchester, Wherwell, or Romsey under pain of a year's confinement at Hyde; particular injunctions were laid down as to eating and drinking; playing at chess or dice was forbidden; frocks or cowls of fustian or worsted were not to be allowed, but were to be of black serge according to their rule; cinctures or burses of silk were forbidden; nor were they to have lockers save in the cloister carols. To this visitation and its consequent decrees the abbot raised formal objections, but he was overruled.

Bishop Orlton visited the abbey on 7 November, 1334, preaching in the chapter-house from 'Ut ambuletis digni Deo per omnia placentes.' The same bishop also visited on 29 May, 1337.

By the aid of 1346 for making Edward the Black Prince a knight we find that the Abbot of Hyde held with Robert Payne an eighth part of a knight's fee in Abbots Worthy (Hidebourne Wordy), three knights' fees in Micheldever, a hide in Northington with Henry de Nonhampton, and half a fee in Bicton with Roger Gervays.

In 1344 there was an outbreak of the villeins of Chisledon, Wilts, against the abbey rule, for which they received chastisement at the abbot's hands. The fearful Black Death of 1349-50 reduced the abbey to penury, so that in order to avoid utter wreck it surrendered itself absolutely into the hands of William Edingdon, Bishop of Winchester and Chancellor of the kingdom. The annalist does not proceed to state what measures the bishop took for the relief of the abbey or how he administered their funds. It would, however, appear that after the election of Thomas de Pechy, the new abbot, in 1362, by good management the monastery had partly regained its prosperous condition, for in 1377 it was able to lend Richard II. the sum of £50. Nicholas Strode who became abbot in 1417 took a considerable share in the political affairs of the day, and is described as 'a man of conspicuous parts and secular activity.' He died in 1440, and was followed by Thomas Bramley, to whose election the royal assent was given early in May. In March, 1446, this abbot's name appears among the distinguished signatories to the final foundation charter of Eton College. In the same year the great bell-tower of Hyde Abbey, with its eight bells, was destroyed by fire. In 1447 Cardinal Beaufort died, and left £200 for the repairs of the church, doubtless in consequence of this misadventure.

Abbot Bramley died in February, 1465, and was succeeded by Henry Bonville, the prior. This election caused much dissension in the abbey.

Bishop Waynflete, on appeal, sent the new abbot to govern the priory of Boxgrove, Sussex, whilst the new prior of Hyde, Thomas Worcester, virtually governed the abbey. In 1471 an arrangement was made by which Abbot Bonville was to receive £50 a year from the abbey revenues, and to attend convocation, council, or parliament as abbot; but he was not to come near Hyde Abbey for three years. Meanwhile however in 1472 Bonville died, and Thomas Worcester was at once elected in his place.

On the election of Richard Hall in April 1488 Henry VII. granted a pension, which a newly elected Abbot of Hyde was bound to grant to a clerk of the king's nomination from the abbey funds, to Peter Carmelian. Peter was a native of Brescia, who had been naturalized that very month; he was a court poet, and chaplain and Latin secretary to Henry VII.

Bishop Wykeham was a firm maintainer of all the episcopal privileges of the See. There was an ancient custom that, on the confirmation of a new bishop, the abbot of Hyde should present him with a choral cope, comely and suitable for a bishop's estate, for use in the cathedral church. On Wykeham's appointment Thomas Pechy, then abbot of Hyde, neglected to supply the customary cope, and ignored frequent reminders. At last, in October, 1368, the abbot was cited to appear in the church of St. Mary Overy to show cause why a cope should not be rendered. The issue is not stated, but doubtless it was in favour of the bishop. In 1390, Bishop Wykeham entered in his register the grant made by Pope Boniface IX. to Abbot Eynesham, authorizing his use of mitre, ring and pastoral staff; on 8 February, 1387, the same bishop issued an elaborate series of injunctions for the better government of the abbey; and by his will left to the abbot a silver-gilt flagon worth £10; to each monk in priest's order, £2 j and to each in lower orders, £1.

Dr. Hede, as commissary for the Prior of Canterbury during the vacancy of the see, visited this abbey on 3 March, 1501. Richard Hall, the abbot, gave written and viva voce answers to the visitation articles. He stated that the abbey was in debt fifty marks when he entered on his office. The common seal was kept under four keys held respectively by the abbot, prior, sub-prior and precentor. Richard Romsey, the prior, said that the abbot had also placed in his hands the office of sacrist. John Lavender, sub-prior; William Salisbury, almoner; Thomas Wrighton, steward; Thomas Gloucester, guest-master; Henry Curtes, precentor; John Forest, cellarer (vinetarius); William Chusylden, the third prior and infirmarer; John Alta, master of the works; William Winchester, sub-chanter; and various others, who did not hold office, summed up their testimony in the effective phrase of omnia bene. Edward London, one of the monks, stated that the novices and two other young brothers did not attend the grammar school, and that it was the fault of the abbot. Anthony Stavely complained that the prior heavily punished the young monks and others without cause. There were also certain complaints on the part of two or three of insufficient food in the infirmary.

Abbot Hall's government was lax. At a visitation held by Dr. Dowman, the bishop's vicar-general, in January, 1507, the prior and six senior monks were summoned to the chapter-house and faced with various serious charges as to the access of women to the precincts, the frequenting of taverns in the city, and insufficient instruction of the younger monks. This was followed by the summoning of twenty-five junior monks who were duly admonished. Then the vicar general conferred with the abbot and seniors as to reformatory measures. The seniors admitted laxity as to egress, alleged their ignorance of all foundation for the graver charges, spoke of the difficulty of a strict observance of the Benedictine rule, but promised vigilance and increased exertion for the future.

Two years later the abbot died, and was succeeded on 19 February by Richard Romsey, the prior, who was the last of the honestly elected abbots of Hyde. He governed the community for nearly twenty-one years under the episcopates of Fox and Wolsey. During the latter part of his life the aged Bishop Fox visited Hyde every fifteen days. In 1522 certain episcopal injunctions were issued which reveal some irregularities, the gravest whereof referred to some of the younger monks practising long-bow archery in the Hyde meadows. In August, 1526, Abbot Romsey received a communication from Wolsey, and wrote asking for a month's time to deliberate over his proposals. He pleaded that he was ' somewhat diseased,' and not well able to travel to see Wolsey, especially as he was expecting the king in the following week. The tenor of Wolsey's letter can be gathered from the reply. He had acknowledged that Romsey had ordered his house 'discreetly as yet,' but now that he was suffering from age and weakness he urged him to resign. The old abbot replied, with some spirit, that he was not so aged or impotent of body or wit, but that he was able to exercise his office to the pleasure of God, the increase of good religion and the wealth of his house.

At the close of 1529 Abbot Romsey died, and on 28 January, 1529-30, the monks of Hyde gathered for the last time in their chapter house for the election of an abbot. A portion of the community struggled hard to appoint one of their own number, but others had been won over to support the election of John Salcot, alias Capon, who was already Abbot of Hulme, Norfolk. After several adjournments, the election of the nominee of Wolsey and the Crown was secured. Salcot was a strenuous and ostentatious supporter of the king's divorce. In 1534 he was consecrated by Cranmer, Bishop of Bangor, and in 1539 translated to Salisbury.

Among all the absolutely unscrupulous turncoats and time-servers of those strange times the last Abbot of Hyde certainly bears the palm. Salcot on his appointment set to work to prepare for the end, and in 1534 or a little later Cromwell designed a strange and most lax regulation for the fraternity; but if ever this came into operation, it was of short duration. In April, 1538, the surrender was signed, and in September of the same year came the visitors, Pollard, Wriothesley and others, vandalizing with their own hands. The number of inmates of the monastery in 1507 was an abbot, a prior, six senior and twenty-five junior monks, making in all thirty-three members.

This number at the time of the dissolution of the house, was reduced to twenty-one. In the eleventh, twelfth and thirteenth centuries, however, it would appear from the lists of admissions to the monastery given in the Liber Vitæ, the number of members was slightly greater. Pensions were assigned to all those who signed the deed of surrender. The abbot's pension probably ceased immediately, as he was rewarded with the bishopric of Salisbury. The prior's pension was £13 6s. 8d. a year; three senior monks had £10 each, two had £8, and the rest £6. Annuities were also granted from the monastic funds to Cromwell, Wriothesley and others. In 1557 there were only the prior and ten of the monks left in receipt of pensions. To Wriothesley were granted some of the richest manors of the abbey, including Micheldever and Stratton, as well as a short lease of the entire site of the abbey, its church and appurtenances. Wriothesley pulled the abbey down with extraordinary rapidity and sold the materials; the reversion of the site, together with the demesne lands, passed by royal grant to Richard Bethell. At the time of the dissolution of the house the monastery held the hundred of Micheldever, the manors of Abbots Worthy,' Slackestede,' Woodmancote, Micheldever with the rectory, c Dottesley,' North Stoneham, * Owers,' East Stratton, Preshaw, Loomer, Alton Eastbrook,

Hyde Abbey Gate ©Stephen Old

'Bicketon,' Brown Candover, Fullerton and Leckford, Abbots Anne, Winterbourne, Pewsey,' Thiseldon with Burythorpp,' Collingborne,

Puddletrenthide, ' Southese, Tytiescombe,' Heighten and Doughton with the rectory. The rectories of Alton, Puddletrenthide and the chapels of Popham, Northampton, Stratton, and lands in Winchester and elsewhere.

When Leland visited Winchester in 1539, so rapidly had Wriothesley done his work that he could find nothing but the site, merely recording that ' in this suburb stood the great Abbey of Hyde.' In Camden's time there are said to have remained some ruinous outhouses, a gateway and a large barn supposed to have been the abbot's hall. William Cole, the antiquary, was here in 1723, and could merely discover the convent barn and holes whence even the foundations had been dug. In 1788 the county magistrates purchased the abbey field as the most suitable spot for the erection of a county gaol ! There seems good reason to

Hyde Abbey Recovered and Reconstructed Arch
©Stephen Old

believe that at this time the grave of Alfred was destroyed and his dust scattered.

The Hyde abbey site was the subject of archaeological digs from 1972 to 1999. The site of the east end of the church was discovered and what was thought to be some of the outbuildings, but none of the claustral complex. It was thought that most of the building. Including the foundations, were removed from site during demolition at the dissolution. The finds from this site are retained at Winchester Museum.

As to the recent archaeological digs, these have been run on a community basis by the community group for the Hyde area of Winchester called Hyde900. They have run a series of community digs from 2016 to 2021 in the gardens of the Victorian terraces that have been built on the site, with the agreement of the house owners. The discoveries made from these digs have re-written much of what was known of the abbey. The layout of the buildings, the scale of the buildings and their decoration has all been reassessed.

As well as excavations, the Hyde900 group have been scouring Winchester for evidence of the re-use of the Hyde abbey building materials, these are called the Hyde Stones and many have been identified in buildings across the city. Another interesting discovery was the finding and identifying of the 13th century roof in Old Hyde House, reused from an abbey building. The only building that was left on the site was the gatehouse and abbey barn which are today the entrance to Hyde Abbey gardens.

One issue with the archaeology on the site, as well as the Victorian houses, is the fact that the site was used for the siting of the gaol or bridewell which would have cut through and disturbed any archaeology that did survive at this site.

Abbots Of Newminster

Grimbald, 903

Beornhelm, Ethelgar, 965-83
Ælfsige, circa 983-97
Brightwold, 995 or 997-1012
Brithmere, 1012-21
Alnoth, 1021-35
Alwyn, 1035-57
Alfnoth, 1057-63
Alwyn II., 1064-66
Wulfric, 1069-72
Rewalan, 1072-
Ranulf Flambard
Herbert Losinga
Robert Losinga, 1091-93
Herbert Losinga, 1093
Hugh, 1100-6
Geoffrey, 1106-24
Abbots Of Hyde
Osbert, 1124-35 (?) Six years' vacancy
Hugh de Lens, 1142-9
Two years' vacancy
Salidus, 1151-71
Five years' vacancy
Thomas, 1177-81
John Suthill, 1181-1222
Walter Aston, 1222-48
Roger of St. Valery, 1248-63
William of Worcester, 1263-81
Robert, or Roger, of Popham, 1282-92
Simon Canning, 1292-1304
Geoffrey of Ferringes, 1304-17
William of Odiham, 1317-19
Walter of Fifield, 1319-62
Thomas Pechy, 1362-80
John of Eynesham, 1381-94
John Letcombe, 1394-1408
John London, 1408-16
Nicholas Strode, 1416-40

Thomas Bramley, 1440-65
Henry Bonville, 1465-72
Thomas Worcester, 1472-9
John Collingborne, 1480-5
Thomas Forte, 1485-8
Richard Hall, 1488-1509
Richard Romsey, 1509-29
John Salcot, 1530-38

The House Of The Franciscans Of Winchester

The Victorian County History starts its section on this house with an assumption that we have read the general section in the book on the Ecclesiastical History of Winchester. There is but little to be added to what has already been stated in the Ecclesiastical History with regard to the coming of the Franciscans to Winchester, their recognition by the bishops as diocesan penitentiaries and preachers, and the dissolution of their house through the agency of the ex-friar Richard Ingworth. Their church was dedicated to St. Francis. The house of the Franciscans or the Friars Minor was located in the north of the old city between what is now Middle Brook Street and Lower Brook Street, south of North Walls.

On 4 May, 1278, the keeper of the forest of Ashley received orders to supply the friars minors of Winchester with four oak stumps for their fuel of the king's gift.

During the episcopate of Bishop Sandale (1316-23), three acolytes, three sub-deacons, one deacon and two priests were ordained from the Franciscan house at Winchester. During the episcopate of Bishop Asserio (1320-3), five acolytes, three sub-deacons, four deacons and six priests were ordained from this convent.

In April, 1330, the pope sent his mandate to the bishops of Winchester, Lichfield and London, directing that the body of Edmund, Earl of Kent, on the petition of Edmund, his elder son, and of Margaret his widow, should be exhumed from the Franciscan church at Winchester and be buried at Westminster; the earl having provided by will that the place of his burial should be left to his widow.

The Franciscans, or 'Gray friars of Winchester,' had their goods appraised at the same time as the Dominicans. The inventory which seems to betoken a larger church than that of the Black Friars, is as follows:—

"A paule and a fruntlet, xijd.; ij alter clothys, xviijd.; iiij crossys, ijs.; ij seynt Johns headys ijd.; j paxe of copper, xvjd.; ij paxyes of wodd, iiijd.; ij pyllows of sylke, viijd.; ij small candelstyckes, xd.; a crysmatorye, 1d.; a desk and a masse boke (nil); ij great candelstyckes, iiijs.; Item an holy-watter stope, xd.; Item a lampe hangynge, xijd.; ij cheyrys for ye quiere, viijd. The Valans. Item a paule and a fruntlet, ijd.; ij altar clothys, vjd.; ij candelstyckes, vjd.

Saynt Clementtes altar. Item a paule and a fruntlet, vjd.; ij altar clothes, vjd.; j candelstycke, viijd.; j payr of crewettes, ijd.

Saynt Fraunces altar. Item a paule and a fruntlet, iiijd.; Item ij altar clothes, iiijd.; a candelstyck, iijd.; ij crewettes, ijd.

In ye vestry. Item xviij corporasseys, iijs.; iij sudorys, iiijd.; ij paules, vjd.; v. fruntlettes, xxd.; j small towell, jd.; Item a cuscheynge of golde, xxd.; Item v settes of vestymenttes, xxviijs.; Item ij syngle vestymenttes of Requiem, iijs.; Item xiiij syngle vestymenttes with amys and without, xvjs. viijd.; A sewt of Requiem without albys, ijs.; Item ij grene tewnakyllys (tunicles) without albys, xvjd.; ij great altar clothys and ij small, xiiijd.; Item vj surples and v coopes, xxxs.; vij lent clothes, vjs. viijd.; ij super altares (nil); Item iiij small albys, xxd.; Item iij flock beddys and a mattres (nil); vj busshels of whete; Item a payre of old organes, iiijs.

Kechyn. Item ix platters, iiijs.; iiij dysshys and iiij sawsers, xxd.; ix eyrye (iron) dyssheys, xvjd.; a chaffer with ij eyrys, ijs. ijd.; Item iij skellets, xxd.; Item iij panys, ijs.; Item ij kettels, xijd.; ij fryying panys, ijs.; Item a chaffer, ijs.; ij broochys, xd.; ij awndyryins, xviijd.; a dryppyng pane, iiijd.; ij trevetts, vjd.; Item ij gyrdyrynes, vjd.; Item ij pothokes, iiijd.; Item iij hangars to

hang pottes on, xijd.; Item a colendar, iijd.; Item a chaffyng dysche, vjd.; Item vj pottes small and great, ixs.; Item a great yren, xvjd.; Item a fumes, vs.
The Buttrey. Item ij tabylclothys and a towell, xxd.
¶In Mayster Denhamys chamber. Item a fether bed a bolster and a coverlet, vs.; Item ij cuschyenes, iiijs.; Item a tester with ij curteynes, xijd.; Item ij baasyns and ij ewers, iijs. iiijd.; Item a pewter bassyn and ij pottes, xijd.; Item iij candelstyckes, xiiijd.; Item a carpett, ijd.; Item a counter, ijs.; Item a cobborde, ijs.; Item a chayre, iijd Summa ixli. iijd."

The above is translated as the following.

"A Pole and a frontlet, 2 alter cloths, 4 crosses, 2 Saint John's heads; 1 paxe of copper1; 2 paxes of wood; 2 pillows of silk; 2 small candlesticks; a chrismatory; a desk and a mass book; 2 great candlesticks; Item an holy-water stope; Item a lamp hanging; 2 chairs for the quire, The Vallance. Item a pole and a frontlet, 2 altar cloths; 2 candlesticks.

Saint Clement's altar. Item a pole and a frontlet; 2 altar cloths, 1 candlestick; 1 pair of cruets.

Saint Francis altar. Item a pole and a frontlet; Item 2 altar cloths; a candlestick; 2 cruets.

In the vestry. Item corpocracy's; 3 sudor;2 poles; v. frontlets.; 1 small towel, Item a cushion of gold; Item v sets of vestments; Item 2 single vestments of Requiem, Item single vestments with amis and without; A suit of Requiem without albes; Item 2 green tunicles without albes, ; 2 great altar cloths and 2 small; Item 5 surplices and v coops 7 lent cloths, 2 super altares (nil); Item 3 small albys; Item 3 flock beds and a mattress (nil); 6 bushels of wheat; Item a pair of old organs.

Kitchen. Item 9 platters; 4 dishes and 4 saucers; 9 iron dishes; a chaffer with 2 ewers; Item 3 skillets; Item 3 pans; Item 2 kettles; 2 frying pans; Item a chaffer; 2 broches; 2 hand irons; a dripping pan; 2 trivets; Item gridirons; Item 2 pot hooks; Item 3 hangars to hang pots on; Item a colander; Item a chaffing dish; Item 6 pots small and great; Item a great iron; Item a fumes.

The Buttery. Item 2 tablecloths and a towel.

In Master Denham's chamber. Item a feather bed a bolster and a coverlet; Item 2 cushions; Item a tester with 2 curtains; Item 2 basins and 2 ewers; Item a pewter basin and 2 pots; Item 3 candlesticks; Item a carpet; Item a counter; Item a cupboard; Item a chair,."

There were debts on the house to the amount of 16s. The site, with those of the other friaries, came into the hands of Winchester College.

The archaeology for this site has been almost impossible as the area is now covered in residential Victorian terraced houses, however, there has been some previous excavation and the results were mixed. The Historic Environment Record (HER) for the site states that "The Friars Minor were established on a plot of land between Middle and Lower Brook Streets, Winchester in 1237; further land was acquired by the Friary in subsequent years. The Friary was dissolved in 1538 when records show that the site contained the church, choir, steeple, cloister, priors lodging, vestry, kitchen, buttery and a chamber. The site was let out in 1539 with all buildings, apart from the Priors lodgings, demolished by 1543 when Winchester College had acquired the site. Various observations undertaken in the 1920's during service installation and other developments have located sections of the precinct wall, features which probably relate to the church and a number of stone coffins. The Priors Lodging was standing in 1856, and Milner traced the church foundations in the great garden between Middle and Lower Brook.

Various architectural fragments, encaustic tiles and other artefactual remains were also recovered. A buried soil located towards the SE corner of the precinct in 2015 during a watching brief may represent a cultivation soil, probably associated with the Friary."

The finds registered in the 2015 watching brief were very few, just enough to show that it was the site of a medieval religious house, with pottery sherds, ridge tiles, peg tiles and oyster shell being the sum total.

The House Of The Carmelites Of Winchester

Of the Carmelite house that stood near that of the Austin friars which was founded in 1278 and dedicated to the Blessed Virgin, there is little to chronicle. Its location was within College Mead between Kingsgate Street and College Meadow, south of the city walls. This area is now part of Winchester College's grounds.

It seems to have been only a small establishment. Bishop Sandale ordained six from this convent, and Bishop Asserio three. The exact location and layout is not known but evidence of it was found in 1871 near Winchester College Infirmary which was built on part of the site. Field observations were carried out at the site in April 1968.

At its suppression in 1538, the dwelling and the land on which it stood only realized a rental of 6s. 8d. yearly.

There is no inventory extant of the Winchester Carmelites. Apparently they were dispersed before Richard Ingworth's visitation.

Female Christian Houses

There was just one known female religious house in Winchester that housed a monastic community, and it was an old and well established house by the middle ages. Unlike the majority of female populated Christian houses, the location of this abbey was adjacent to the cathedral, nearly all others were located in more rural environs,

Nunnaminster, Or The Abbey Of St. Mary, Winchester

The buildings of the Nunnaminster no longer exist and are partially buried under the Gothic Revival Victorian Guildhall building that was built between 1871 and 1873 and is still in full use today. The original buildings would have been of wood and probably thatched, but was rebuilt during the Norman period in stone and gradually added to until the dissolution.

Burials at Nunnaminster

Some archaeological remains are visible in the area adjacent to the guildhall, in Abbey Passage, the result of archaeological digs in 1973 which exposed the frater range including the vaulted undercroft and 1981-3 which exposed the church nave as well as other key finds including burials and a staff of office that would have been carried by the abbess.

To the north-east of St. Swithun's, and immediately to the east of the New Minster, stood the great abbey of St. Mary, the nuns' minster, usually known as Nunnaminster. It was founded jointly by Alfred and his queen Eahlswith, about the close of the ninth century, but the buildings were completed by their son, Edward the Elder. After Alfred's death, the queen retired to this monastery, where she died. It would seem probable that she should have been made abbess, but Leland describes Edburga the daughter of Edward, who died in 925, as the first abbess.

The endowment of the monastery seems to have been inadequate for its maintenance, and it is said to have fallen into great poverty. King Edred bequeathed to it Shalbourn and Bradford in Wiltshire; but notwithstanding this addition to its revenues, Bishop Aethelwold, possibly on account of its poverty but more probably with a view of establishing there the stricter form of Benedictine rule, practically re-founded it in 963, and apparently re-endowed it.

By the Domesday Book we learn that the abbess held Lyss, Froyle, Leckford Abbess, Long Stoke, Timsbury, and Ovington in Hampshire; Coleshill in Berkshire; and Urchfont and All Cannings in Wiltshire. We know nothing of the history of this monastery from this date till the middle of the twelfth century, when during the civil war between Matilda and Stephen the city of Winchester, together with this monastery, was burnt in 1141. It was a rule that upon the election of an abbess, the convent was bound to find, in early times, a corrody and later a pension for a person nominated by the Crown, and in this way it appears that Juliana de Leygrave, niece of the king's (foster) mother, Alice de Leygrave, who suckled him in his youth, received at the election of Maud de Pecham in 1313 a nun's corrody for life, the value to be received by her wherever she might be, and a suitable chamber within the nunnery for her residence whenever she might wish to stay there. This prerogative of the Crown seems to have been exercised at each election of an abbess, and writs for the payment of such corrodies or pensions are to be found among the public records. The Crown also seems at a later date to have claimed a right to nominate a nun for admission to the monastery at the coronation of each sovereign, and a like privilege was exercised by each Bishop of Winchester at his consecration.

Besides the professed nuns and their household the abbey of Nunnaminster supported a certain number of chaplains or canons who had prebendal stalls in the abbey. The original idea of having canons attached to these old Benedictine foundations seems to have been to provide the nuns with suitable chaplains, as well as with priests who could superintend the management of their temporalities. The canons of Nunnaminster could, however, as a rule, have been of little or no service to the monastery, whose income they drained. For instance, at his own request, the pope granted Roger Holm, canon of this monastery in 1349, the church of Elvydon, in the diocese of Salisbury, notwithstanding that he was also the holder of canonries in Lincoln and London, and was expecting a benefice from the Abbot of Ramsey. Or again, Canon Richard of Norwich of this convent had papal sanction in

1355 to hold a London canonry, although in addition to the prebend from Nunnaminster he drew the emoluments of prebends from Salisbury and Kilkenny, and held the church of Adesham.

Throughout the papacy of pope Clement VI. (1342-52) pluralism was specially rampant, and there were few worse cases than those of the holders of prebends in the Hampshire nunneries of Nunnaminster, Romsey and Wherwell.

In 1317 papal sanction was obtained for Roger de Inkepen, a wealthy and beneficent citizen of Winchester, to found and endow a chapel in the cemetery of Nunnaminster, to be served by two priests, the patronage of which was to belong to him and his heirs. This chapel was dedicated to the Holy Trinity; one of the priests was termed the warden and the other the chaplain; they lived together and had a common table; they were ordered to say daily mattins and evensong in the chapel in addition to the masses.

In December, 1321, this chapel was defiled by shedding of blood, when the bishop commissioned Peter, Bishop of Corbavia, to reconcile it. We have mention also of another chantry in the monastery founded at the altar of St. Peter at the east end of the south quire aisle by Robert de Wambergh, Archdeacon of Wells, in 1328. It was endowed with lands at Urchfont for the support of a chaplain to pray for the souls of Emeline Longspee and others.

During the fourteenth and fifteenth centuries the abbey, like other similar foundations, seems to have got into pecuniary difficulties. In 1343 the convent attributed one of the chief causes of their poverty to the action of the king in taking the profits of the temporalities during a vacancy, and to assist them they petitioned the pope for licence to appropriate the parish church of Froyle. To this the pope assented, but ordered that it should be done through the diocesan. The preliminary arrangements for this appropriation had been carried out by Bishop Orlton just before his death; but on the succession of Bishop Edingdon, that prelate, with the support of the Archbishop of Canterbury, refused his sanction. Whereupon the convent in 1346 again approached the pope, setting forth the state of affairs, and pleading the sterility of their lands, the destruction of their woods, the diminution of their rents, and the excessive number of nuns and sisters, whereby they were unable to pay their debts, provide for the inmates, or repair the buildings. They further pleaded the reduction of their temporalities through royal administration. The pope in reply empowered the Bishop of Hereford to carry out the appropriation. In the same year Bishop Edingdon issued an inhibition to the abbess not to receive sisters beyond the ancient number.

A few years later in 1349 the monastery suffered on account of the Black Death. The abbess, Maud Spine, apparently succumbed to this plague, at all events there was a vacancy in that year. The cattle plague which followed the Black Death severely affected the convent. This, coupled with the general reduction of their rents and the barrenness of their lands, caused by the sparsity and dearness of labour, were among the causes again pleaded on behalf of Nunnaminster, in a petition to the pope in 1352, for the appropriation of the church of Gretford, in the diocese of Lincoln, valued at 40 marks. The prayer was granted, and the ordinance of the vicarage was committed to the Bishops of Salisbury, Worcester and Wells.

Notwithstanding that the custody of the temporalities during a vacancy was granted to the prioress and convent at a rent to the Exchequer in 1464, which, as we have seen, was a concession much sought after by the convent, the abbess and convent in 1468 again complained that they were so burdened with the repair of their houses and church, and with the payment of tenths and other imposts that they could not fulfil the obligations of their order as to hospitality. To assist them in their distress King Edward IV. granted that they should have view of frankpledge and assize of bread and ale, with waif and stray at their towns of Urchfont and All Canning's, in the county of Wilts, from all their tenants and other residents. In 1476 a further grant was made, as the previous one was not so valid as had been hoped, that the nuns should have all sums of money and rents due to the king from themselves or their tenants or other residents in the same towns.

On 24 January, 1370, the bishop excommunicated certain persons who had been instrumental in the abduction of one of the nuns; and in June of the same year he issued his mandate to the abbess to re-admit a nun, Isabel Gerway, who had apostatized, but was then anxious to return. The name of the abducted nun is not given in the first of these documents, and they both probably refer to the same sister.

Some idea as to the internal rule of the house can be obtained from the frequent visitations of the bishops of the diocese. In 1308 Bishop Woodlock commissioned Lawrence, sub-prior of St. Swithun, and Master Stephen de Dene, his commissary general, to visit the nunnery; on 16 March, 1309, he issued an elaborate series of injunctions for the better government of the house, divided into thirteen heads. Bishop Stratford (1323-33} also held, or caused to be held, various visitations of his monastery, and on two occasions cited the Abbess Maud for the correction of excesses.

It is recorded that Bishop Orlton (1333-45) personally visited Nunnaminster on 9 April, 1334, when he preached in the chapter house from the text, ' Deo per omnia placentes.' In 1336 he commissioned his official to visit for the correction of excesses (the usual phrase), and there was a further visitation in 1337. Bishop Wykeham paid considerable attention to the monastery. In 1384 he addressed a mandate to the abbess for the correction of nuns who were disobedient to their officers, and censured the superior for lack of discipline. In September, 1396, the bishop commissioned Nicholas Wykeham, Archdeacon of Wilts, and John Elmere, the official, to visit the abbey, and on 14 June, 1403, he granted his licence to the abbess and nuns to hear divine service in their new Lady Chapel adjoining the quire. By his will Wykeham left to the abbess five marks, and each of the nuns one mark.

Dr. Hede visited St. Mary's on 2 March, 1501, when Abbess Joan Legh washable to give satisfactory evidence as to the order and administration of her house. The common seal was kept in a chest, the three keys of which were in the respective possession of the abbess, prioress and sacrist. Margaret Fawcon, the prioress, testified that all the sisters had their meals in the frater, save one who was very aged. Agnes Tystede, sub-prioress, testified that all the convent rose at night for mattins, save the sick and aged. Christiane Whytyngton, infirmarer, stated that the annual balance sheet was duly presented in chapter. Margaret Bawdewin, precentor, testified that omnia bene (all was well). Agnes Trusset, the second cantor, Agnes Kyng, the third cantor, and Agnes Massaw, the fourth cantor, gave brief evidence to the same effect, and so also did Alice Tystede, scrutator, Agnes Byrcher, Margaret Shafte, Agnes Cox, senior teacher (dogmatista), and Margaret Legh, mistress of the novices. Elia Pitte, the librarian, was also well satisfied with that which was in her charge.

The first commissioners appointed for visiting the Hampshire monasteries were Sir James Worsley, John and George Poulet, and William Berners. Their report of St. Mary's, Winchester, was highly favourable. They visited this nunnery on 15 May, 1536, and examined on oath Elizabeth Shelley, the abbess; Thomas Lee, auditor; Thomas Legh, receiver; and Thomas Ticheborne, clerk. They found in the convent 102 persons, namely, 26 religious, 5 priests, 13 lay sisters, 9 women servants, 20 officials and waiting servants, 3 corrodiers (pensioners), and 26 children. Their names are all set forth in full. Of the religious persons, all, save four, were professed, and ' every of them intend to keep their habits and religion to what house religious or ever they shall be committed by the kings highness, Dame Frith Welbeck only excepted, who desired than to be committed to any other house to have capacity.' All the professed are termed Dames. The five chaplains were Master John Hazard, confessor, and four others.

Among the women servants were Jane Sherley, ' the abbas gentlewoman,' as well as a servant. The prioress, sub-prioress and ' sexton ' (sacrist) had each their servant in their respective houses, and so had 'Dame Maud Burne in her house.' The other three were ' lavenders ' (washerwomen) to the abbess and convent. The officials and servants were a general receiver, clerk, ' curtyar ' (curtiler), cater, butler, cook, under-cook, baker, convent cook, under convent cook, brewer, miller, porter, under-porter, porter of Eastgate, two ' churchmen,' ' Peter Tycheborne child of the high altar,' and two servants of the receiver and clerk respectively. The corrodiers were Thomas Legh, John Lichfeld and Richard Yeckley.

The twenty-six ' children of lords, knights and gentlemen brought up in the said monastery ' were: ' Bridget Plantagenet, daughter unto the lord viscount Lysley; Mary Pole, daughter unto Sir Geoffrey Pole knight; Bridget Coppeley, daughter unto Sir Roger Coppeley, knight; Elizabeth Philpott, daughter unto Sir Peter Philpott knight; Margery Tyrell; Adrian Tyrell; Johanne Barnaby; Amy Dingley; Elizabeth Dingley; Jane Dingley; Frances Dingley; Susan Ticheborne; Elizabeth Ticheborne; Mary Justyce; Agnes Alymor; Emma Bartue; Myldred Clarke; Anne Lacy; Isold Applegate; Elizabeth Leigh; Mary Leigh; Alienor North; Johanne Sturgess; Johanne Fielder; Johanne Francis; Jane Rainsford.'

The commissioners put on record that the religious persons of this house 'have been and are of very clean, virtuous, honest, and charitable conversation, order, and rule since the first profession of time, which is also reported not only by the Mayors and Community of the City of Winchester, but also by the most worshipful and honest persons of the Centre adjoining thereunto, which have daily made a continual suit unto the said Commissioners to be suitors unto the King's highness for toleration of the said monastery.'

'Item the said monastery is in a very good state of Reparation and stands nigh the middle of the City of a great and large com passe environ with many poor household is which have their only living of the said monastery, and have no demands whereby they may make any provision but live only by their hands, making their provision in the markets.'

They returned the monastery as out of debt, and reported that the convent seal was put in a bag sealed with the seal of Richard Poulet, locked in a coffer with three keys, which remained in the custody of the abbess and two of the chief governors of the monastery; that the value of the lead on the church and houses was £154 10s., and there were five great bells and one little one, worth £28 2s. 6d.; that the inventory of the jewels, ornaments, household stuff, stock and stores amounted to £486 13s. 7d.; that £24 6s. 8d. was owing to the monastery; that the annual value of the lands and possessions was £330 18s. 6¼d., and that the value of the woods was £231 6s. 4d.

The Valuer of 1535 returned the gross annual value of the abbey as £245 17s. 2½d., whilst the clear value was only £179 7s. 2d., which brought it well within the limit of the Act of the following year for the suppression of the smaller monasteries. It is difficult to account for the great discrepancy between this valuation and that made by the commissioners in 1536 as given above even after making allowance for the former being an assessment value. It was possibly owing to this higher estimate that St. Mary's escaped the destruction of those houses whose revenue was less than £200 per annum, but more particularly on account of the payment of the great sum or bribe of £333 6s. 8d. On 27 August, 1536, letters patent placed the establishment on a new and diminished foundation, the Wiltshire manors of Urchfont and All Canning's being granted to Sir Edward Seymour (Viscount Beauchamp) and Anne his wife. Elizabeth Shelley was at the same time confirmed in her position as abbess.

But the respite was not for long. In September, 1538, Cromwell's commissioners proceeded ' to sweep away (from St. Mary's) all the rotten bones that be called relics.' At last, on 15 November, 1539, the Surrender ' was signed, before Robert Southwell and other commissioners, pensions being granted to the abbess of £26 13s. 4d.; to the prioress, £5; to two nuns, £4; to two, £2 16s. 8d.; and to seventeen others, £2 13s. 4d.

In the following years these pensions were confirmed, as well as 6s. 8d. each to twelve poor women called sisters, and the Site granted to John Bello and John Brarholme. The ' houses' that were recommended to be ' sustained ' were the abbess' lodging, stretching from the church to the frater on the north, with its court and appurtenances, the buttery, pantry, kitchen and larder; the gatehouse; the barn; the bakehouses; the brewhouse; the garner; the stables; and the mills. Among the superfluous buildings was of course the church, and also the cloister, chapter house, dorter, frater, infirmary, convent kitchen, the two garners on the south side of the court, the priest's lodging and the plumber's house. The lead on the church, quire, aisles, steeple, cloister and other houses was estimated at 220 fothers (1 fodder = 19.5 hundredweight). There were five bells, but no 'jewels.' There were 118 ounces of plate, and the ornaments, goods and chattels had been sold for £69 15s. 4d.

At the time of the dissolution of the monastery the possessions included the manor of Froyle with the rectory, the manors of Itchen, Leckford Abbess, Timsbury, Greatford with the rectory, and Braceborough, and lands, rents, etc. in the city of Winchester, Lyss Abbas, Wetham, Godsfield, Shamelhurst, Swindon, 'Hacheborne,' Shipton Moyne, Blandford and ' Barnethorpe.'

In the days of Camden, at the beginning of the seventeenth century, there were considerable remains of the Nunnaminster; but now no traces of it exist save the name and certain watercourses. It stood between High Street and Colebrooke Street.

Abbesses Of Nunnaminster

Edburga, died 925
Ethelreda, 963
Edith, in the time of King Edgar
Beatrice
Alice, 1084
Avice, 1120
Clarice, 1174
Agnes, 1236-64
Euphemia, 1265-70
Lucy, 1270-87
Christine de Winton, 1287-99
Agnes de Ashley, 1299-1313
Maud de Pecham, 1313-37
Maud de Spine, 1337-49
Margaret Molins, 1349-64

Christiane Wayte, 1364-5
Alice de la Mare, 1365-85
Joan Denemede, 1385-1410
Maud Holme, 1410-4
Christine Hardy, 1414-8
Agnes Denham, 1418-49
Agnes Buriton, 1449-86
Joan Legh, 1486-1527
Elizabeth Shelley, 1527-39

The Harley Manuscripts

The Harleian library was founded in October 1704, when Robert Harley (1661–1724) purchased more than 600 manuscripts from the collection of the antiquary Sir Simonds d'Ewes (1602–1650). In 1711, Harley was elevated to the peerage as 1st Earl of Oxford and Mortimer, from which date his son, Edward Harley (1689–1741), was most active in augmenting the collection. The 1710s saw further groups of important English manuscripts enter the library, and from about 1717 the Harleys also began using overseas agents to make en bloc purchases of manuscripts from Continental Europe, especially France, Germany and Italy. Numerous important British and foreign collections were auctioned in London in the 1720s, allowing further individual acquisitions. Edward Harley, 2nd Earl of Oxford and Mortimer, maintained a wide circle of friends, among them the writer Jonathan Swift (1667–1745) and poet Alexander Pope (1688–1744).

A prominent role in the formation and expansion of the library was played by the scholar Humphrey Wanley (1672–1726). Wanley, one of the original members of the Society of Antiquaries in 1707 (re-founded in 1717), became library-keeper to the Harleys in 1708. His diary and letters are an important resource for describing the acquisition of individual manuscripts, and for understanding the growth of the collection as a whole.

Edward Harley bequeathed the library to his widow, Henrietta Cavendish Harley (née Holles), countess of Oxford and Mortimer

(1694–1755), during her lifetime, and thereafter to their daughter, Margaret Cavendish Bentinck, duchess of Portland (1715–1785). In 1753, the manuscripts were sold by the Countess and the Duchess to the nation for £10,000 (a fraction of their contemporary value) under the Act of Parliament that also established the British Museum.

Chapter 3 – Christian Hospitals

Medieval hospitals were nothing like what we call a hospital today. They were houses, often religious but also secular; there for any traveller or pilgrim, to provide shelter and sustenance but often with another function, to provide support for the local community. This is a function that those that are still in existence today have retained, mostly in the form of charitable accommodation in the form of Almshouses.

Set up by rich benefactors, these hospitals sprung up in many towns but especially those that were a site of pilgrimage like Winchester. Their founding was to meet a need and to prevent hardship among the poor, pilgrims and travellers, to prevent them being taken advantage of by local tradespeople of less than charitable intent. Space was limited and often reserved to the most in need. There are records of five such hospitals in the city of Winchester, two of which survive to this day, St Cross and St John

The Hospital Of St. Cross, Near Winchester

The far-famed hospital of St. Cross, which still stands about a mile from Winchester, between the Itchen and the Southampton road, was founded between 1132 and 1136 by Bishop Henry de Blois.

The small chartulary, or register of St. Cross, still extant, gives copies of two bulls confirming the foundation of the hospital; one was granted by Pope Innocent II. in 1137, and the other by Pope Lucius II. in 1144. The charter of the founder delivered to Raymond, prior of the Knights Hospitallers, the hospital founded for the weal of his soul and those of his predecessors and the kings of England, and provided for the reception, clothing and entertaining of 'thirteen poor impotent men, so reduced in strength as rarely or never to be able to raise themselves without the assistance of another.' In addition to this a hundred other poor men of good conduct were to be entertained daily at dinner, and permitted, on departure, to take away with them the remnants of both meat and drink. The first master mentioned, in a grant of Bishop Blois, was Robert de Limosia.

Serious disputes arose with respect to this hospital during the next episcopacy (Richard of Ilchester, 1174-88), between the bishop and the Hospitallers. At length, on 10 April, 1185, the Order formally gave up the management to the diocesan, by which agreement the bishop undertook to provide daily for 200 men instead of the original 100. The chartulary shows however that the Order of Hospitallers did their best to recover the management, and actually obtained two papal awards in their favour of the years 1187 and 1189. In 1197, Pope Celestine III. commissioned the Bishops of London and Lincoln and the abbot of Reading to settle the dispute, and they gave their award in favour of the bishop. Nevertheless, only two years later King John again confirmed the hospital to the Hospitallers.

Church and Ambulatory St Cross Hospital ©Stephen Old

The decision however of the papal commissioners was upheld, and in 1204 the Bishop of Winchester appointed a master, which right has since been maintained by the bishops down to the present day. The

Hospitallers nevertheless clung to the muniments and records until 1379, when the energetic Bishop Wykeham obtained them from Prior Robert Hales. The prolonged dispute as to the valuable patronage of this hospital had seriously impeded the intentions of the founder, and delayed its completion. The great church was not finished until the year 1255, when special appeals were made for assistance.

The gross mismanagement of this grandly conceived foundation, and the alienation of so large a share of its funds from the poor to wealthy pluralists, which made the mastership of St. Cross a scandal and a byword for full six centuries, began at an early date.

Brothers Accommodation Wing St Cross Hospital ©Stephen Old

On 16 June, 1321, the Bishop of Winchester received orders from the king to induct the king's clerk, Geoffrey de Welleford, to the house of St. Cross, which he had deferred doing, although he had verbally admitted Geoffrey at the king's presentation; pretending that the house was filled by Robert de Maidstone, the king having ordered him to admit a suitable person notwithstanding the claim of the late Bishop of

Winchester, because the king had recovered in his court the presentation by reason of the late voidance of that bishopric. The obedient prelate duly inducted Geoffrey, for the second time, by proxy, on 26 June. This was followed on 28 June by a more imperative order to the bishop, telling him to certify by the bearer if any further resistance should be offered; as the king was informed that when the bishop ordered his commissary to induct Geoffrey's proctor, the commissary found many persons at the house who actively resisted him so that he could not execute the order. The resistance continued, and on 3 July the bishop made a third induction of Geoffrey, with a solemn warning to all who should resist. On 12 July the sheriff of Hampshire was ordered to take with him sufficient power of the county, and to go in person to the house of Holy Cross, and to the churches annexed thereto, and to remove all lay or armed force from the house and churches, and to put Geoffrey de Welleford in possession.

He was further instructed to imprison any one resisting the execution of the order. In this mandate it was also recited that the sheriff's bailiff had reported that he visited the house on Friday after the Translation of St. Thomas to remove all lay or armed force, and that he found no force nor resistance, and therefore did nothing in the matter, 'at which answer the king marvels, especially as it is testified before him by trustworthy men that a lay and armed force was then and is still in the house of St. Cross, and that the bailiff's answer was made frivolously and derisively.' The king's next step, in this determined assertion of his authority and rights, was to prohibit the archbishop from attempting anything prejudicial thereto. A further writ on the same subject was addressed to the archbishop on 23 October. On 4 September a commission of oyer and terminer was granted on the complaint of Geoffrey de Welleford, that, after due induction, Robert de Maidstone, Nicholas his brother, and divers other persons, had taken and carried, of the hospital property, livestock to the value of £100, goods and chattels to a like amount, as well as charters and muniments. A second commission, dated 6 November, particularizes the missing property, and increases its value to the then great sum of £500.

The bishop, on 9 February, 1322, issued a commission of inquiry relative to the dilapidation of St. Cross on the entry of Geoffrey de Welleford. On 11 March, Geoffrey, by proxy, promised canonical obedience, as master of St. Cross, to his diocesan. Geoffrey, who had been thus stormily thrust into this valuable mastership, died in August, 1322, having never apparently set foot in the diocese. Bishop Asserio was now able to make an appointment of his own; but it was no improvement on that of the king. His choice for this valuable and important preferment fell on his nephew, Bertrand de Asserio, a clerk of the diocese of Cahors. He was collated, inducted and instituted (by proxy) on 31 August, 1322, by his brother Gerald de Asserio, vicar-general, in the absence at the Roman court of the bishop. There seems no reason to imagine that Bertrand ever saw the hospital of which he was the master, although he held it with a rectory in the diocese

Ambulatory and Gate To Garden St Cross Hospital ©Stephen Old

(Freshwater, Isle of Wight), and a prebend of Salisbury. In August, 1330, Bertrand, as warden of St. Cross, nominated attorneys to act for him, as he was going across the seas for two years.

Provision of the hospital was made in 1333, by Pope John XXII, to Peter de Galliciano, void by the resignation of Bertrand de Asserio, who had exchanged it for other benefices out of England. Meanwhile Bishop Stratford endeavoured to checkmate the papal appointment by sequestrating the hospital property on the ground of the blindness and inability of the new master, and there ensued a strife between ecclesiastical and civil authorities to the great bewilderment of the tenantry, the sheriff being called upon in October, 1334, to assist Peter de Galliciano, the master, in levying rents due to him.

In 1344, the bishop petitioned Pope Clement VI., signifying that when the hospital of his collation was vacant, he made provision of it to William Edingdon, the king's treasurer, who restored the buildings and improved the condition of the poor therein, spending £1,000; but on the report that the late Peter de Galliciano, master of the hospital, was chaplain to Clement V., and that the hospital was therefore reserved to the pope, of which the bishop was ignorant, he prayed the pope to declare valid the appointment of William and all that he had done. To this the pope assented, and remitted the fruits he had received. In the following year Edingdon became bishop, and the pope appointed Raymond Pelegrini, papal nuncio, to the mastership of St. Cross, which was declared to be worth £6 13s. 4d. (fn. 20) Raymond resigned in 1346, and was followed by Richard de Lusteshall and Walter de Wetwang; both of which appointments were brief and disputed.

In 1346 Bishop Edingdon appointed his nephew John Edingdon, a mere lad, to the mastership, who of course neglected all the duties pertaining to his office as grossly as his predecessors. Provision was made in June, 1348, of the hospital by the pope, to William de Farlee, notwithstanding his holding canonries and prebends of Winchester, Romsey and Salisbury. But in 1349 the bishop signified the pope that he had given St. Cross to John Edingdon, his nephew, who was under age, and already held two benefices, there being an ordinance in the foundation that it could be given to secular clerks; but that as it was reported that the pope had reserved the same before Richard's death, he prayed him to confirm the collation. The petition was granted.

In 1366, Edingdon, having stripped the hospital and its estates, resigned, soon after his uncle's death, and was followed, on exchange, by William Stowell, who in his turn exchanged the mastership in March, 1368, with Richard de Lyntesford, for the rectory of Burghclere. In August, 1370, Lyntesford exchanged the mastership with Roger Cloun for the rectory of Campsall, Yorkshire.

The scandals of St. Cross were now to be arrested. Bishop Wykeham was a very different diocesan to his predecessors. Stowell resigned on 22 March, 1368, and on the following day the bishop demanded of him an inventory of the stock received by him from Edingdon and handed over to Lyntesford. The story is a piteous one; whilst episcopal and royal and papal nominees to this benefice were spending the hospital's incomes in their own selfish ways, the great hall had fallen in, the hundred poor were ejected from their daily meal, and the thirteen infirm inmates were turned away to seek shelter where they could.

From 1368 to 1375 Bishop Wykeham, with rare persistency, followed up the iniquities of the four living masters, and at last gained the victory. On 6 January, 1375, Cloun made his submission to the bishop, and swore he would render an annual account to his diocesan whenever called upon to do so. The bishop however was now strong enough to refuse the master any power of administration, and put in a relative of his own, Nicholas Wykeham, to superintend the affairs of the hospital. By this arrangement further peculation was prevented, the buildings began to be repaired, and the endowments mainly used for the poor. In 1382, Roger Cloun, the nominal master, died, and Wykeham appointed his great friend John de Campeden, rector of Cheriton, to the mastership.

Wykeham's successor, Cardinal Beaufort (1404-47), with the consent of Thomas Forest, then master, and the brethren, added, in 1445, to the original foundation a hospital or Almshouse of 'Noble Poverty,' the buildings of which were to be erected to the west of the church. The troublous times and the triumph of the Yorkists prevented his intentions being carried out in his lifetime, and it was left to Bishop Waynflete to further to some extent the cardinal's intentions. The bishop procured an enabling charter in 1455, but it was not until 1486 that he carried out his plan and remodelled the statutes. The cardinal's intended endowments were lost, which meant that the additional foundation, designed for two priests, thirty-five brethren and three sisters, was reduced to one priest and two brethren. Those of the new foundation wore a cloak of deep red with a cardinal's hat embroidered in white; whilst those of the old foundation retained the black cloak, with silver cross-potent, as ordained by the Hospitallers.

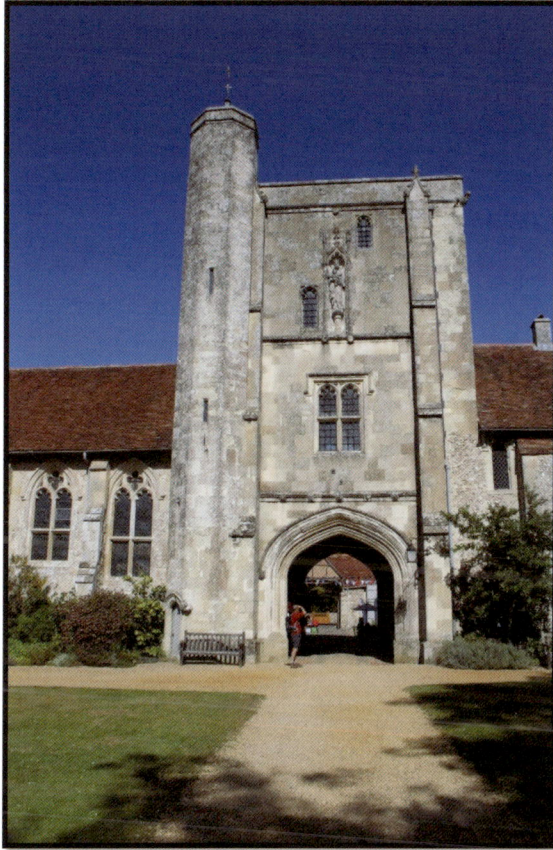

Beaufort Tower St Cross Hospital ©Stephen Old

The Reformation made but little change at St. Cross. The hospital, though threatened in the time of Henry VIII, luckily escaped confiscation. At a visitation held by Dr. Legh, as Cromwell's commissary, in 1535, it was directed that the thirteen brethren should receive sufficient meat and drink and not money in lieu thereof, and that the 100 men be daily fed, but sturdy beggars repulsed.

It was further ordained that some discreet and honest priest of the house should hear and teach the poor brethren the Our Father and the Creed in English, which they were to say together in the church before dinner; that the master was to have a library in the house which was to contain printed volumes of the Old and New Testaments and the works of Jerome, Augustine, Theophylact and others of the most ancient fathers; and that mass was to be said for the soul of the founder and for the good estates of the king and Queen Anne.

In 1696, when Dr. Markland was master, it was alleged that all documents and registers pertaining to the hospital had been burnt, and a 'customary' (consuetudinarium) was drawn up by the master for its future management, and ratified by the bishop. When the scandals of the abuse of this charity were brought before the Queen's Bench in 1851, the judge in delivering judgment described this 'customary' as a 'barefaced and shameless document' and 'a wilful breach of trust.' He was equally severe on the nineteenth century continuation of the scandal. The present wholesome scheme was devised in 1855-7.

As the site is still fully in use and is still a vibrant institution there has been very little in the way of Archaeology required to tell the story of this hospital, however, in 2008-10, WARG (Winchester Archaeological Rescue Group) undertook community excavations in the park adjacent to the current precinct and in 2013 WARG undertook an excavation of the bowling green area adjacent to the church.

The 2008-10 digs were investigating the lumps and bumps in St Cross Park to work out what they related to. The report is still being produced but the basic outcome was to show that there was a water feature, probably fish ponds and that the Lockburn that goes through the site was diverted and culverted to refresh these fish ponds. The Lockburn, which rises in the centre of Winchester and was the main city drain,

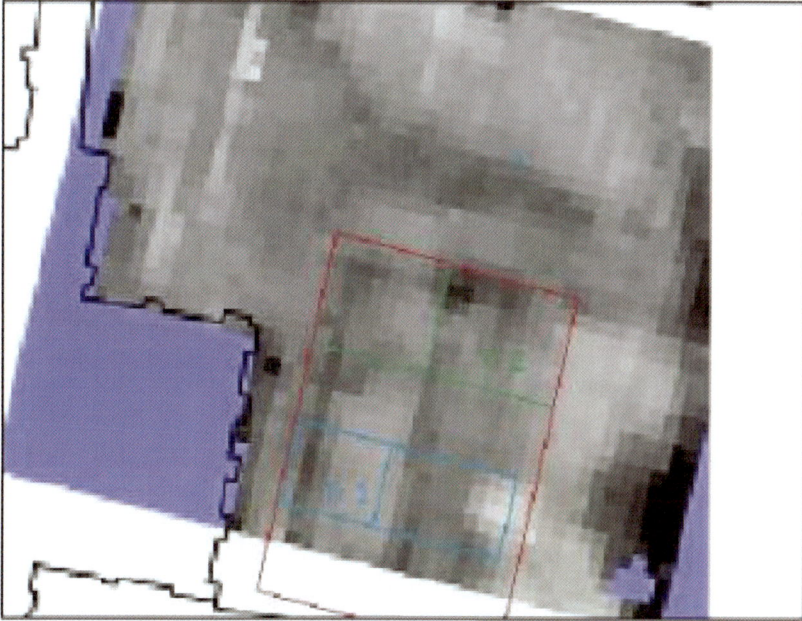

St Cross Hospital Bowling Green GeoPhys ©WARG

St Cross Hospital Bowling Green Black & White Tlie Floor ©WARG

passes underneath the western range of St Cross Hospital and the waste from the inhabitants would have been deposited into it from their toilets. The Lockburn eventually reaches the river Itchen just south of the Hospital site.

The 2013 dig had the aim to find evidence of the original hospital building from the founding in 1132-6 as this area seemed to be the most promising. A geophysical survey was done with the help of the University of Winchester and a hazy outline of a possible hall was revealed. This helped WARG target where on the site they could concentrate their resources.

The full dig report is again still awaited but the dig was a success in proving the existence of the original hall, with two entrances, being about the same size of the hall at Wolvesey Castle (Old Bishop's Palace) which was built about the same time. Also revealed were a set of black and white floor tiles in situ, two clear doorways, one quite functional and the other much grander, internal rooms and some quite interesting finds like a pilgrims ampulla that was used to carry holy water.

Masters of The Hospital of St. Cross, Winchester

Robert de Limosia, 1136 ?
Roger, 1185
Alan de Sancta Cruse, 1190
Alan de Stoke, appointed 1204
Henry de Cusia or Susa, appointed 1241
Geoffrey de Fernyng, appointed 1250
Thomas de Colchester, appointed 1260
Stephen de Wotton, died 1275
Peter de Sancta Maria, archdeacon of Surrey, 1289-96
William de Welynger or Wendling
Robert de Maidstone, 1305-20
Geoffrey de Welleford, 1321-2
Bertrand de Asserio, 1322-33
Peter de Galliciano, 1333
William de Edingdon, High Treasurer of England, 1335-45
Raymond Pelegrini, papal nuncio, 1345-6
Richard de Lusteshall
Walter de Wetwang
John Edingdon, 1346-66
William Stowell, 1366-8
Richard de Lyntesford, 1368-70
Roger de Cloune, 1370-82
John de Campeden, 1382-1426
John Forest, 1426-44

Thomas Forest, 1444
Thomas Chandler, warden of New College, 1463-5
William Westbury, provost of Eton, 1465
Richard Hayward, died 1489
John Lichfield, 1489-91
Robert Sherborne, 1491-1500
Richard Fox, Bishop of Winchester, 1500-17
John Claymond, President of Magdalene and Corpus Christi Colleges, appointed 1517
John Incent, appointed 1524
William Meadow, 1545
John Leefe, 1557
Robert Reynolds, 1557
John Watson, 1559
Robert Bennett, 1583
Arthur Lake, 1603
Sir Peter Young, 1616
William Lewis, 1627
John Lisle, 1649
John Cooke, 1657
Richard Shute, 1660
William Lewis, 1660
Henry Compton, 1667
William Harrison, 1675
Abraham Markland, 1694
John Lynch, 1728
John Hoadley, 1760
Beilby Porteus, 1776
John Lockman, 1788
Francis North, 1808
L. M. Humbert, 1855
W. G. Andrewes, 1868

The Hospital Of St. Mary Magdalen, Winchester

The original site of the hospital of St. Mary Magdalen was about a mile due east of Winchester, on the down which was called after it,

Magdalen Hill, now Morn Hill, a derivation. It does not seem to be possible to trace its first foundation with any certainty, although the cumulative presumptions in favour of Bishop Ilchester (1174-89) being the founder, ingeniously put forth by Dr. Milner, seem highly probable. Moreover the elaborate drawings made of the remains of its chapel by Mr. Schnebbelie, in 1788, corroborate this view, as they show that the main work was apparently late in the Norman style. The first mention of the hospital occurs in the register of Bishop Pontoise (1280-1304), where it is named in a list of benefices of which the Bishops of Winchester had been patrons for a long time. It is mentioned once in Stratford's register, under the year 1325, when it is called a hospital for lepers. Pope John XXII. in 1333 granted a faculty to the prior and chapter of Winchester to appropriate the church of Wonsington, value £40, out of which, however £25 19s. 4d. was to be paid yearly to the hospital of St. Mary Magdalen, according to the prescription of Henry, late bishop of the see. The foundation at that time consisted of a priest (master) and nine poor brethren and nine poor sisters.

On 8 September, 1334, the keepers of the temporalities of the see of Winchester, then in the king's hands, were directed to pay to the master and paupers of the hospital of St. Mary Magdalen on the hill, the arrears of a certain fixed sum for their maintenance, as they had been in the habit of receiving such a sum during voidance from the king's progenitors. In 1336 the taxers and collectors of the tenth and fifteenth in Hampshire were ordered not to molest or aggrieve the master and brethren of the hospital, and to permit them to be quit for that turn, as the hospital was so slenderly endowed that its goods hardly sufficed for the maintenance of the master, brethren and sisters, and of the weak and infirm there, and for other alms according to the foundation.

From Bishop Orlton's registers the interesting fact is established that it was at one time customary for the bishop to collate not only the master, but the various inmates of the house, whether brothers or sisters. Thus in 1338 Bishop Orlton collated William de Berwick to a portion or share in the house, with all its rights, customs and pittances. In 1339 the bishop collated Margaret Greenway to another portion, which had been held by Henry le Bule, clerk, whilst he remained in the hospital.

In 1342 the same bishop collated William de Basynge, clerk, to the perpetual custody of the hospital, assigning to the custodian or master four 'greater portions. Both in Orlton's and Wykeham's registers the chapel of St. Mary Magdalen is termed a chantry, in consequence of the obligations that rested on the priest and brethren and sisters to pray for the souls of the founders and of all the faithful departed.

According to Trussell's MS. history of Winchester, 'The House of St. Mary Magdalene was founded by Maria de Valentia, daughter of Guido, Earl of St. Paule of France, wife of Adamore de Valentia, Earl of Pembroke, in the days of Edward the Third.' This is of course incorrect, but it may quite possibly refer to some special benefaction, or scheme of re-founding. Certain it is that there was a considerable architectural reconstruction of the hospital in the first half of the fourteenth century.

In 1394, John Melton, who was the first schoolmaster of Winchester College, was collated by Bishop Wykeham to the wardenship of the hospital and chantry, to which, as again stated, was assigned the share of four 'greater portions.' The form of collation reminded the new master of his obligations, for therein is reference to the Quia contingit bull of Clement, whereby he was bound to make an annual return of the goods and expenditure of the hospital. In the following year the bishop, on the death of William Chaloner, one of the brethren, collated Roger Muleward to his place; John Melton, the master, was ordered to induct the new brother. Much earlier in his episcopate (1369), Wykeham had collated to this hospital one Adam Coudrich, who is described as aged, weak, poverty stricken, and unable with his own hands to gain a maintenance.

Wykeham was as keen to check abuses on a small scale as those on a larger throughout his diocese. Encouraged by the successful issue of his contention with the great hospital of St. Cross, he next turned his attention to the much humbler foundation of St. Mary Magdalen. On 1 September, 1400, he appointed John Campeden, Archdeacon of Surrey, and Simon Membury, treasurer of Wolvesey, two of his most trusted friends, as commissioners, with full power to visit and inquire into the condition and administration of this hospital. The report showed that many 'delinquencies, crimes, and excesses, had been brought to light; and Wykeham' on 20 November of the same year, commissioned Campeden and Membury, together with John Elmore, his official, to punish canonically the offenders, and even to expel the master, or any other delinquent, if justice required it.

Among the Harley Manuscripts is a portion of a rental of the hospital, with an inventory of the furniture of the chapel and house, taken about 1400. The receipts were: £25 19s. 4d. from the treasurer of Wolvesey; £6 9s. 4d. from the prior of St. Swithun's; 22s. from the abbot of Hyde; 60s. from the bailiffs of Winchester; and 16s. 3d. in rents—yielding a total of £37 6s. 11d. These receipts were thus allotted. The sum from Wolvesey was for eighteen persons, 5d. a week each for victuals, and 6s. a year each for clothing. From the entries already cited in the registers of Orlton and Wykeham, it would seem that four of these portions were allotted to the master, and that would reduce the other inmates to fourteen, or seven of each sex. It is quite clear from this and other documents that the episcopal founder of this house originally designed it for eighteen inmates, nine of each sex, and that by the fourteenth century a reduction to fourteen, in addition to the master, had been accomplished. The sum from St. Swithun's was assigned to ten persons, 3d. a week for each, namely three farthings on Sunday and on three week days, and nothing for clothing unless the convent, for love of God, gave them some old clothes. It would seem as if this pension, when originally granted, was intended for the partial relief of ten persons outside the bishop's eighteen. From the same source were supplied four flitches of bacon, namely one on each of the eves of Christmas, Ash Wednesday, Easter and Pentecost. The money from the bailiffs and from Hyde Abbey was for the general support of the brethren and sisters. There were also for the support of the house 14 acres of land, and pasturage for 101 sheep in the pasture of St. Swithun.

The oblations received at the chapel on the festival of St. Mary Magdalen were reserved for the repairs of the house and the walls, save 13s. 4d., which was assigned for the reaping and carrying, of their corn. Offerings made at other times were divided equally among the inmates.

The warden's stipend is named as consisting of four of the greater portions, that is of those provided from the Wolvesey bequest, and came to £5 15s. 4d.

The ornaments of the chapel included in addition to chalices, crosses, vestments, etc., a rochet for (the image of) Magdalen; an old missal; a new one worth 100s., the gift of William Basinge, a former master; a great noted portifer, worth 60s.; two old antiphonars; a legendary of the saints; a calendar (temporal'); three psalters; a collectary; a hymnary; a manual and three graduals; a green carpet powdered with birds and roses; and five banners for carrying at Rogation-tide. The inventory of the brass and pewter in the domestic buildings mentions six houses, besides the master's house.

The visitor, according to the list of questions, was to inquire if the chaplain (master) duly celebrated and said the canonical hours; if he lived chastely and soberly and visited the sick and punished delinquents; if he wasted the hospital's substance, or allowed any destructions of houses or trees; and if he reproved evil livers; whether husbands and wives were cohabiting in the hospital or had a house there; if the clerk served the church and chaplain with due obedience; whether there were any living in common, or in separate houses using their portion in any bad or extravagant way; if there was any one disobedient, or quarrelsome, or wandering contrary to the statutes; whether the goods of a deceased inmate went to the works of the church after the payment of debts; whether any one was unwilling to submit to the justice and discipline of the master; whether any brother or sister was not living in Christian peace; and finally whether any one entered into the house save through the treasurer of Wolvesey.

It seems highly probable, as the rest of this MS. book pertains to Wykeham, that these are the very list of questions drawn up for the guidance of his commissaries in 1400. From a study of them it seems obvious that there were at that time six houses, in addition to the master's house, in which lived those inmates who drew major portions, as well as others, namely the ten provided for by the St. Swithun's pension, who lived in a common hall and dorter.

The exact issue of Wykeham's inquiry and correction cannot be now ascertained; but it is fair to assume that the condition of the hospital was materially improved, otherwise he would scarcely have made the hospital a bequest in his will, which was drawn up about two and a half years after the inquiry had been held.

Among testamentary bequests to this hospital may be mentioned 6s. 8d. in 1420, by John Fromond, steward of Winchester College under Wykeham, the words of whose will are: Lego ad distribuendum inter leprous B. Marie Magdalene, Wynton. This need not however be taken to prove that the brothers and sisters were all, or even any of them, lepers. Like many another hospital founded for the relief of lepers, as the disease disappeared the inmates were selected from other poor and impotent folk. The Valor of 1535 gave the gross income as £42 16s. William Atkinson was at that time master.

Hospitals were not included in the Act of Edward VI. for the dissolution of chantries and other like foundations, and therefore St. Mary Magdalene's does not appear in the certificates taken under this Act, but in the certificate of 1545 its value is entered as £41 6s. 8d., of which £19 7s. 4d. was divided amongst nine poor men and women. After other payments, there was a balance left for the master and the repair of tenements of £13 9s. 4d. The certificate states that the hospital was founded by the Bishop of Winchester 'to pray for the souls of their founders and all Christian souls.' The great reduction in numbers from eighteen to nine is not such a flagrant instance of mismanagement or peculation as might at first seem to be the case. By far the larger part of the hospital's income came from fixed pensions, and the purchasing power of money had certainly lessened by one half in the course of three and a half centuries.

Dr. Ebden, master of the hospital, by indenture dated 2 September, 1611, gave £10 annually to be divided at the rate of 4d. weekly to each of the brethren and sisters, and a gown each at Christmas.

At the time of the great Civil War the hospital suffered severely from the king's troops. Out of its little flock of sheep thirty-six were killed by the soldiers, and the remainder had to be conveyed away sixteen miles for safety. Much corn was stolen, and the great gates, doors, barn and stable fittings, in short everything of wood was burnt. Even the furniture of the chapel down to the very holy table were used for fuel, and horses of the troopers were stabled in the sanctuary. The master, brethren and sisters petitioned Lord Hopton, general of the Royalist forces in the west, as to the destitution and misery brought on the inmates. In an order dated 19 March, 1643, the general promised inquiry and redress.

The master and poor folk had not long been in their renovated houses, when the government of Charles II., in 1665, chose to seize it as a place of confinement for the Dutch prisoners of war, and to order that the alms folk were to be removed into lodgings at Winchester at the king's expense. The result was most disastrous; the Dutch prisoners used all the woodwork, including that of the restored chapel, for fuel; and the chapel bell, and all iron and lead were carried away. In short, the hospital was ruined; and the master, brethren and sisters found it impossible to return when the war was over. The estimate for rebuilding and repairing was £650, but the government would only allow £100. Dr. Gulston was at that time master. His successor, Dr. Darel, who was also archdeacon of Winchester, purchased, in 1671, some tenements for the poor outcasts in Colebrook Street, which were left after his death in trust for the use of the hospital. In 1788 the remnants of the old buildings, including the beautiful chapel, still bearing many traces of wall painting, were pulled down, and the materials used for the erection of six plainly built Almshouses on the upper side of Water Lane, in the East Soke.

The old buildings are fully described as well as illustrated in the Vetusta Monumenta. A view of their original state is given at page 155 of Mr. Wavell's second volume, before referred to, wherein are shown the chapel with master's house and common rooms adjoining, together with the range of small houses for those who held the major portions.

Archaeological excavations have been carried out on the site through

St. Mary Magdalen Dig from the Air ©WARG

the years but most recently by the University of Winchester and in particular Simon Roffey since 2007, after the Channel 4 Television programme "Time Team" started an investigation in 2000. They have now started to investigate the sites more recent past when it was used as one of the largest troop transit camps during WWI and was then known as Morn Hill Camp.

Radio carbon analysis at this site, the former Leper Hospital at St Mary Magdalen in Winchester, Hampshire, has provided a date range of AD 960-1030 for a series of burials, many exhibiting evidence of leprosy, on the site. This makes it one of the earliest hospital sites known in England and shows the site was occupied as a leper hospital before the later Norman rebuilding and re-founding. This also shows that Leprosy was present in the population pre Norman.

Masters of The Hospital. of St. Mary Magdalen, Winchester

William de Basynge, collated 1342
John Melton, collated 1394
William Waynflete, 1438
William Atkinson, 1535
Dr. Ebden, 1611
Dr. Gulston, 1665
Dr. Darel, 1671
Mr. Wavell, 1773

The Hospital Of St. John Baptist, Winchester

St Johns is one of the surviving hospitals in Winchester but is now a charity that provides housing for those in need with premises across the city. Some of the original hospital buildings can be seen in The Broadway, opposite the Victorian Guildhall, and in the areas between The Broadway and Friarsgate/Eastgate Street. Most of the original buildings have changed use through the ages. It has a friendly rivalry with The Hospital of St Cross who both claim to be the oldest charity that has had continuous patronage

When Leland visited Winchester, about 1538, he saw near the east gate 'a fair Hospital of St. John, where poor sick people be kept. There is in the Chapel an image of St. Brinstan, sometime Bishop of Winchester: and I have read that St. Brinstan founded a Hospital in Winchester.' This supposition of so exceptionally early a foundation, though frequently copied as a fact into guide books and local histories, seems to have been a mere guess of Leland's suggested by the sight of the image of Bishop Brinstan.

The real history of the hospital begins with the foundation, about 1275, by John Devenishe, alderman of Winchester, of a hospital or hospice for the relief of sick and lame soldiers, poor pilgrims and wayfaring men, to receive there gratuitous food and lodging for one night or longer, according to their ability to travel. He endowed it competently, and furnished the rooms with bedding and other necessaries, and made the mayor custodian to regulate admission to its privileges. The founder attached a chapel to the house, and therein established a priest to celebrate for his soul and for all the faithful departed. About fifty years later one of the same name as the founder, probably his son, made a further bequest to the chaplain of the house, and added to his duties.

In January, 1332, licence was obtained by John Devenysh for the gift of 100s. of rents in Winchester and Little Somburne, to the master and brethren of the hospital of St. John, to find a chaplain to celebrate daily in the hospital for the souls of the king's progenitors, kings of England, and of the faithful departed.

Mark le Faire, who was mayor of Winchester in 1408 and subsequent years, was a benefactor of the hospital, giving it a part of the George inn, the King's Head, and his own house. At this time the hospital was in the full control of the corporation, for in 1408 an order was made by the assembly that the house of St. John Baptist should be rebuilt during the year and roofed with lead. The cost was to be partly defrayed by voluntary contributions, for the gathering of which the assembly appointed two collectors.

It appears from the Black Book of Winchester that town assemblies were frequently held here in the fifteenth and sixteenth centuries. The Trussell manuscripts state, indeed, that this use of the hospital hall for municipal purposes was coeval with its foundation. 'It appears by the book of ordinances of this city (earlier than the extant Black Book) that in the time of Roger le Long, who succeeded John Devenishe in the place (as alderman), that there was an ordinance made that every year, upon the next Sunday after Midsomer day (except upon some extraordinary inane occasion hindered, and that not to be allowed of but by a general assembly), the mayor and his brethren and all the whole corporation with their wives should meet at this house at supper, whereat over and above the rate set, the mayor for the time being, and he that was mayor the precedent year, were to bestow a couple of fat capons; which love-feast and merry meeting was appointed to revive the memory of the Devenishes. This meeting is observed to this day.' From the same authority we learn that Richard Devenish increased the endowments in the reign of Henry VI.

John Trussell (1575-1648) was a collector and collator of historic documents. He had a business in Winchester and was also involved in local politics, becoming an Alderman of Winchester and serving as Mayor in 1624 and again in 1633. John Trussell used his documents and his further research to write several books on national history and local history including a history of Winchester.

At an assembly held on 20 August, 1442, as chronicled in the Black Book, it was resolved that the chaplain of the fraternity of St. John was to receive meat and drink and sufficient cloth for a gown (toga) yearly from the steward of the fraternity, and four marks as a stipend.

The corporation in 1442 appointed William Wyke, clerk, as chaplain and keeper of the hospital, and caused the following indenture of the hospital's goods to be drawn up. From the provisions for bedding, it would appear that the house had not given up the exercise of nightly hospitality for wayfarers.

The present indenture bereth Wittness yt Petur Hulle mayre of ye Cite of Wynchester and All ye Commoners of ye same Cite hath delyvered to Sr William Wyke oure keper of oure hous of Synt Johns of Wynchester al oure goodes and catelles underrite, Firste viij corperas, iiij tuellis for ye autres in ye churche goode, and v holde, ij litel tuelles for ye lavytory olde, j paxebrede of silver and over gyld a j nother paxbrede, and a hede of Syn John ye Baptis of Alabastre, j Box of silver wt oute over gylde, ij chales of Silver wtynne over gylde, j chales of silver ye gylde w oute, ij ymages of Syn John ye Baptis of Alabastre, j ymage of oure Lady of Alabastre, v chopis (copes) of sylke and a litel pelow, viij proper vestements wt all ye apparell, ij surplis feble, j aube wt parurys, j Crystal stone, j Box wt dyvers reliquis, iij Missales, ij Antiphones, ij portions, vj sawters, ij legendes, ij Grayellis, j episteler, j marteloge, and vij other diverse bokes, iiij sakeryng belles, iiij cruettes, ij lamps of brasse, j mettable (dining table) w ij trestallis, ij belles for ye churche wt j Trunke, pond' viijc, j forme, ij meteclothis conteynynge in lenthe xiiij yerdes wt a towell conteynyng in lenth iij yerdes and a halfe, ij Basonis and j laver, j litel morter of Brasse for Spices to pounde on weying xij lb., iiij bras pottes, j belle and j litel pomette, j hangynglaver, xj payre of Shettes, iiij payre blanketts, xxiij keverlytes, j crowl, j spade, j shovell, j howe, j rake, j spytele, j Longpyke, j whelberewe, j bounde wt Ire, ij cofor in ye chambers wt munnimentes and chartes.

This translates, as well as I can make out to the list below

"The present indenture bears Witness that Peter Hull mayor of the City of Winchester and all the Commoners of the same City has delivered to Sir William Wyke our keeper of our house of Saint Johns of Winchester all our goods and chattels underwritten, First 8 corperas, 4 tulles for ye altars in ye church good, and 5 holder, 2 little tulles for the lavatory old, 1 paxebrede of silver and over gild a 1 other paxbrede, and a head of Saint John the Baptist of Alabaster, 1 Box of silver without over gilded, 2 challis of Silver within over gilded, 1 challis of silver the gild without, 2 images of Saint John the Baptist of Alabaster, 1 image of our Lady of Alabaster, 5 copes of silk and a little pillow, 8 proper vestments with all ye apparel, 2 surplice feeble, 1 aube with parures, 1 Crystal stone, 1 Box with diverse reliquiae, 3 Missals, 2 Antiphons, 2 portions, 6 salters, 2 legends, 2 Grails, 1 epistler, 1 martelog, and 7 other diverse books, 3 sakering bells, 4 cruets, 2 lamps of brass, 1 mettable (dining table) with 2 trestles, 2 bells for the church with 1 Trunk, pond' 1 form, 2 meat cloths containing in length 14 yards with a towel containing in length 3 yards and a half, 2 Basins and 1 laver, 1 little mortar of Brass for Spices to pound on weighing 12 lb., 4 brass pots, 1 bell and 1 little pomette, 1 hanging laver, 11 pair of Sheets, 3 pair of blankets, 23 coverlets, 1 Crowl, 1 spade, 1 shovel, 1 hoe, rake, 1 spittle, 1 Long pike, 1 wheelbarrow, 1 bound with Iron, 2 coffer in the chambers with muniments and charts."

The next entry in the Black Book, immediately following this inventory, is the record of a meeting of the assembly in the house of St. John Baptist on 31 August, 1485. Other meetings of the Corporation in the same hall are recorded in 1472, 1514, 1520 and 1523.

At an assembly held in the guildhall on 6 January, 1524, there was 'granted to my lord Suffragan Saint John's house with the garden for time of his life yielding yearly for the said house 16s. 8d. and for the garden 10s.' Ten years before his death, which occurred in 1528, Bishop Fox suffered from blindness. Much of the diocesan work was discharged by John Pinnock, Bishop of Syene, who also acted as suffragan Bishop of Salisbury.

At an assembly held in St. John's Hall on 2 March, 1531, it was ordained that 'from henceforth every Maire in his time shall examine the Inventory of all the church goods of Saint Johns and all other goods belonging to Saint John's hospital within 3 months next after the feast of Saint Michael the archangel upon pain of forfeiture of 6s. 8d. to the use of the City.'

At an assembly held on 23 April, 1535, 'hit is granted to Richard Frankelyn, servant of the said City, to have the oversight and keeping of Saint John's house and the hospital there as long as it shall please the mayor and the City to admit him.'

The assembly of 8 August, 1546, decided 'that the supper accustomed to be kept at Saint John's house shall from henceforth yearly be kept there the Sunday next following the Nativity of Saint John the Baptist in as ample manner as it hath been here to fore And every of the bench shall pay at the same supper 12d. and every other of the 28s 10d. apiece, and of the other franchise man 8d. apiece, and that whether they be present there at the supper or not. And the mayor for the time being to find a capon at the same supper and the alderman of the High Street another capon.'

At the dissolution of such institutions in 1546, this hospital fell into the hands of Henry VIII., but it was not altogether suppressed, and was by him regranted to the corporation, the hall to be used by them for municipal elections and the like purposes. At that time the hospital revenue was but 100s. a year, 30s. of which was for the priest's stipend.

In 1558, Ralph Lamb bequeathed £400 to the master and brethren of this hospital, for the purpose of adding to it as many poor as the rents of the lands purchased with the bequest would maintain, who were to be called 'The Alms folk of Ralph Lamb.' An estate was purchased at Amesbury, Wilts, as well as some small properties in Winchester, and six poor and needy widows were established in as many Almshouses in a court on the north side of the main building.

In the charter which was granted by Elizabeth in 1588 to the corporation, this hospital, with the addition of the Lamb Almshouses, was confirmed to them as its keepers.

In an old account book of the corporation, beginning about 1688, the Charity Commissioners (in 1824) found an entry, under the title of 'The poor of St. John's hospital weekly,' of the names of twenty-two persons, men and women receiving 6d. a week each, and of six others receiving 1s. 6d. each per week, the latter being probably the alms people appointed under Lamb's gifts. At the time of the Commissioners' visit, there were no other alms folk nor any doles to the poor save those on Lamb's foundation.

In 1811 a suit was begun against the corporation for mismanagement and abuse of this and other charity trusts. After almost continuous litigation for nearly twenty years, the corporation surrendered, and in 1829 resigned their powers and responsibilities to the trustees appointed by the Court of Chancery.

After the Reformation, when the chaplain's stipend was appropriated, the chapel was disused. It was rescued from its ruinous condition in 1710, and turned into a schoolroom for sixty poor children. It was used as a school until 1838, when it was repaired and restored to its original use.

St. John's House, with its fine hall and chapel, still stands at the east end of the High Street, and behind it are twenty-one commodious Almshouses.

St Johns House, Broadway

The Sustern/Sustren Spital

This small hospital was located on the south side of College Street, next door to Jane Austen's house and with Winchester College (St Mary's) on the other side. This was outside the city wall but still close to the cathedral, access to the cathedral being via Kings Gate which is close by.

This Hospital was in existence by 1148 and was a sisters hospital, it was sometimes known as the Sisters Spital, that belonged to the Cathedral Priory. It consisted of a hall, chapel, chambers and a kitchen. It is mentioned in 1352-3 and 1387 in connection with victims of the Black Death. It next appears in the 18th century when it was rented by Winchester College as lodgings for commoners (boys who were not scholars). In 1808 and 1837 Winchester College acquired the freehold.

At this point it was merged with Winchester College, the building outlines still exist though their use has altered over the years since. There is not much actually written about this particular institution so one can surmise that it's path through the centuries was uneventful, being an integral part of the cathedral and controlled through the cathedrals hierarchy. It was dissolved in 1539 under Henry VIII.

Christ's Hospital

Although founded much later than the others, it has a medieval base to its foundation. Christ's Hospital was founded in 1607 by Peter Symonds, a Native of Winchester and afterwards a Mercer in the City of London. and is located in Symonds Street (1-7) which is close to the cathedral and inside the city walls. Dated 1607 on stone in South gable end, but altered in the late 19th century.

The building is of two storeys except the centre gable on the East front, which has 5 storeys. It is constructed of red brick with stone quoins and blue brick patterns on a flint base. The Central East gable has been rebuilt. The Ground floor Has eight windows and five doors, the first floor has eight 8 windows. The windows are all casements, with 19th century plain wood frames, two and three-light, four-light in the centre. The doorways are arched. The building has a Tiled roof with Good original stacks in red brick set diagonally on stone bases at the rear. The number "7" has been added in grey brick in the mid-19th Century.

On foundation, the Endowments of this House for the maintenance of Six Old Men, One Matron, and Four Boys, and also to the Assistance of One Scholar in each of the Two English Universities (Oxford and Cambridge). By agreement this charity was absorbed by St John's hospital and the buildings are now looked after by the St John's hospital board.

Chapter 4 – Christian Colleges

The original meaning and use of the word "College" simply applies to places where a community or body of clergy live together supported by a foundation and can apply to an educational establishment or to a chantry training establishment. The words use has changed over the centuries and now only applies to an educational establishment. Winchester had one of each type, with just one surviving to the modern day.

The two Winchester colleges were very different both in regime and size, but at the dissolution, it was the larger and more influential one that came through and took over not just the other college but also many of the other Christian houses in Winchester

The College Of St. Elizabeth, Winchester

The Victorian County History article on St Elizabeth's College starts with a description of its location. Near to the gate of his castle at Wolvesey, Bishop Pontoise built, in 1301, the college of St. Elizabeth of Hungary. The foundation consisted of a number of secular clergy and choristers living under the rule of a provost, with so clearly an expressed' object that it was in reality a chantry on a large scale. In the episcopal registers and other documents, it is most usually described as the chapel of St. Elizabeth, but frequently as a college and sometimes as a chantry.

By the foundation charter, the bishop established three altars in the great chapel. The dedication of the high altar was to the honour of St. Elizabeth; the second to the honour of St. Stephen and St. Laurence; and the third to the honour of St. Edmund and St. Thomas of Canterbury. To serve these altars and to maintain a stately ritual, the foundation provided for the establishment of seven chaplains, one of whom was to be provost, three were to be in deacons' and three in sub-deacons' orders. All were to be appointed, as vacancies occurred, by the bishop; they were to live together and have a common table; to be satisfied with one dish and pittances on week days and two dishes on

Sundays and double feasts; to dress humbly, and to wear in chapel surplices and black copes; to receive annually in addition to their board for clothes and other necessaries: the provost 6 marks, the chaplains 40s. and the clerks 20s.; to have a common dorter for the clerks save in sickness; each chaplain to have a young shaveling, between the age of ten and eighteen, to wait on him, and to sing in surplice in church; and the choristers to dine together in hall at a separate table. Their clerical duties were to rise each day at daybreak and say together (submissa voce aperte et distincte) mattins of our Lady, and afterwards to chant antiphonally mattins of the days; after mattins to celebrate solemn Lady mass after the use of Sarum; next to intone the proper day hours, followed by the hours of our Lady in a low voice; immediately afterwards, the mass of St. Elizabeth was to be sung, followed by the saying of three masses at the three altars, two for the departed and one of the Holy Spirit; and about nine o'clock high mass was to be solemnly sung. Each chaplain was to say at each mass six special collects (1) for the founder, (2) for the then Bishop of Winchester, (3) for all the departed bishops of the diocese, (4) for the king and queen and their children, (5) for kings and queens and all faithful departed, and (6) a general collect for the quick and dead, but especially for the prior and convent of St. Swithun's. Before evensong, all the chaplains and clerks were to say, in low but distinct voice, Placebo and Dirige; afterwards to say evensong of our Lady, and to sing evensong of the day, to be followed by compline of our Lady and compline of the day.

Everything was to be according to the use of Sarum; the provost and chaplain were to appoint one of their number as precentor, to order the masses and services. The provost, in the presence of the chaplains and the treasurer of Wolvesey, was yearly at Winchester to deliver a statement of account, and a report as to the condition of the chapel and house. No one was to be absent from masses or hours save by special leave. No chaplain or clerk was to be admitted, unless first examined in letters and singing, and in knowledge of the divine offices. Women were not to enter any part of the house, save the chapel and hall. Each chaplain and clerk on admission was to swear to be faithful to the statutes and rules, and to continue in personal residence.

The original endowment included the appropriation of the church of Hursley and 6 acres in the meadows of St. Stephen where the college stood. Soon after the foundation, Simon de Fareham gave to the college the manor and church of Botley. Other gifts were the manors, etc., of Kingsclere and 'Culmestone Gynninges,' and lands at Shedfield. John de Wynfred was the first provost appointed by the founder.

In 1307, Edward II. inspected and confirmed the letters patent of his father confirming the foundation charter of the chapel of St. Elizabeth with the chapel of St. Stephen; and at the same time confirmed to Richard de Bourne, the provost, and the chaplains and clerks, the grant of appropriation of the church of Hursley, which had been made without the licence of the late king.

In February, 1313, licence was obtained sanctioning the gift to the college of the manor of Norton St. Walery by Robert de Harewedon, clerk, and William de Stamford. In the following April, the provost and chaplains of St. Elizabeth were excused the service of rendering yearly a sore sparrow-hawk for the manor of St. Walery, at the request of Hugh le Despencer the younger, of whom it had been held in chief by that service.

Bishop Asserio collated priests, deacons and sub-deacons to the chapel of St. Elizabeth, and Peter, Bishop of Corbavia, held ordinations in this chapel, on behalf of the Bishop of Winchester, on 21 November and 18 December, 1322, and also on 19 February and 12 March, 1323. The ordination of 18 December was a large one, there being 75 acolytes, 27 sub-deacons, 36 deacons and 47 priests.

We find that in 1346 the college held one knight's fee in Norton and Sutton Scotney, a twelfth part of a fee in Clerewodcott, one fee in Culmeston and half a fee in Botley.

In 1350, Bishop Edingdon, in direct contravention of his predecessor's statutes, obtained the papal sanction for John de Nubbelaye, rector of Alresford and canon of Romsey, to hold the provostship of the chapel, together with his rectory and canonry, as the income of the chapel was too small to be held by itself.

Bishop Edingdon, when ratifying to the college the gift of Hursley church, contrived in some way to secure to himself and successors the rectory house. The possession of the rectory was however restored to Provost John de Sheptone and the chaplain by Wykeham in 1373, when the college undertook to pay an annual pension of 13s. 4d. to the bishop.

In September, 1400, the bishop commissioned John Elmore, the official, and Simon Trembury, treasurer of Wolvesey, to visit the college.

After the death of Bishop Wykeham, the provosts of St. Elizabeth were in the main non-resident and the holders of other preferments. The college of St. Elizabeth was visited on 4 March, 1501, by the commissary of the prior of Canterbury, during the vacancy of the see. The visitation entry merely states that Richard Wilmer, precentor, appeared as proctor for Richard Newport, the provost, and gives the names of five chaplains, five clerks and seven choristers who were present.

When the Valor of 1535 was taken, 'Doctor Pers' (Peers) was provost; the gross annual value was declared at £120 0s. 8d. and the clear value at £112 17s. 4½d.

On the dissolution of this college among the smaller houses, in 1536, it formed one of the numerous grants made by Henry VIII. to Thomas Wriothesley, who sold the site to the warden and fellows of Winchester College for £360.

Leland describes the college of St. Elizabeth as 'situated East upon the New College; and there is but a little narrow causeway between them. The main Arm and Stream of Alresford Water divided a little above the College into 2 Arms on each side of the College. Within these 2 Arms not far from the very College Church of St. Elizabeth is a Chapel of St. Stephen.'

Mr. Kirby describes the acquisition of this site by Winchester College as a piece of good fortune. It stood in what is now the warden's kitchen garden, facing the cloisters. On the ordnance map, in the meadow near the school bathing place, is marked 'site of St. Elizabeth College'; but the foundation of an oblong building on that site really belonged to the chapel of St. Stephen.

When Wriothesley sold St. Elizabeth's to Winchester College, he imposed a condition that the buildings should be either pulled down or converted into use as a grammar school before Pentecost, 1547. In the deed of sale, 18 April, 1544, the college of St. Elizabeth is described as having a church, belfry and cemetery, and containing 4½ acres. Possibly there may have been originally some idea of turning St. Elizabeth's into a boarding house for scholars; but within a year of the purchase the new owners began the work of demolition, stripping the lead from the church, and using the stones for building the wall which bounds the south side of Meads.

A rather clumsy fifteenth century oval seal represents St. Elizabeth of Hungary standing in a canopied niche, with a palm branch in the right hand and a book in the left. Behind her is an angel with extended wings holding a crown over the saint's head. The idea of this seal is far better than its execution. Legend: s' COMMUNE · COLLEGII · SANCTE · ELIZABETH.

In 2011, 2012 and again in 2014 WARG (Winchester Archaeology and Local History Society) carried out archaeological digs on the site of St Elizabeth's College. The full reports on these digs are still in production as the findings from the dig are quite significant so there is a need for extensive reports from various experts. Probably because the college was relatively short lived, the preservation of the tiles, masonry and some metalwork is so good as to be of national importance. What was found is the compacted chalk raft, the line of the foundations including the main doorway and the possible location of the three known altars.

Due to the sites nature, being on a flood plain of the River Itchen, excavation was sometimes difficult due to the ingress of water, this was

0 5 10 20 30 40 Meters

GeoPhys Results St Elizabeth College ©WARG

especially true of the burials that were found within the chapel chancel area which soon became waterlogged in rainy conditions.

The Geophysical Survey, carried out with the assistance of The University of Winchester clearly shows the outline of the building including where buttresses were placed.

College Of St. Elizabeth, Winchester Provosts

John de Wynfred, 1301

Richard de Bourne, 1307
Adam de Capel, 1316, 1317
Nicholas de la Flode, 1320-2
John de Gorges, 1322
John de Thynd, 1334
John de Nubbelaye, 1350
John de Peveseye
John de Sheptone, 1373
Thomas Boys, 1381-7
John de Ketone, 1387
Simon Wylet, 1387-97
John Hulyn, 1397-1401
Walter Hardene, 1401
Richard Newport, about 1501
Dr. Pers or Peers, 1535, 1536

St. Mary's College or Winchester College/School

A full description of this colleges main campus is also the start of the article on Winchester College in the Victorian County History. Immediately south-west of Wolvesey Palace in the southern suburb of the ancient city is the College of St. Mary, founded by William of Wykeham in 1387 on a site bought of the Prior and convent of St. Swithun, outside the jurisdiction of the mayor and corporation and within the bishop's own jurisdiction of the Soke.

The original plan of the College consisted of three quadrangles, Outer Court, Chamber Court, and cloisters, one beyond another and successively smaller: Outer Court containing the business premises, Chamber Court the living rooms, and cloisters, approached through the chapel, the final resting-place of the society. In this state they remained for a century and a-half without addition. At the Dissolution the college underwent expansion, taking in three or four more quadrangles. It occupied the site of St. Elizabeth's College on the east, which was eventually annexed by the warden for his house and garden; its Commoners found extended premises in the Sustern Spital, a hospital for women, a dependency of the monastery on the west, and the garden or playing-fields called Meads were extended at the expense of the Carmelite convent on the south. In this state things continued for another hundred years. In the 17th century, before the Civil War, Sickhouse was built on the actual site of the Carmelite Friary, and after the erection of School there was added a fourth quadrangle called School Court. In the middle of the 18th century the Sustern Hospital was finally consolidated and annexed under the name of Commoners' College with its two quadrangles, now represented by Moberly Court and Flint Court. For a century again expansion ceased. Then, not long after the middle of the 19th century, Commoners were once more shifted westward. First came sporadic houses, one in St. Thomas' Street (now being moved to Kingsgate Park), another in Kingsgate Street, and another on Southgate Hill, nearly half a mile away. A little later almost a new Commoners' College sprang up in the four houses clustered together on Culver's Close with a fifth opposite them in Southgate Street. A gate was cut in Meads' Wall, and Meads became a long, irregular quadrangle of grass bounded by the river and the road, taking in successively Lavender Meads, New Field, and Dogger's Close. A mistake was committed towards the end of the century, when the college declined to expand to the north by annexing the 17th-century house of Wolvesey and the ruins of the residence of the founder, with its beautiful grounds between the city wall and the cathedral. A ninth house was added in 1907 in Kingsgate Park and a tenth, in the same park, is now (1911) just finished.

Winchester College. Argent two chevrons sable between three roses gules, which are the arms of William of Wykeham, the founder.

The stern, unbroken line of frontage which the college presents to the outer world when approached down College Street, past the head master's house, has precisely the same fortress-like aspect as when it was first erected outside the city walls, with the dangers of sudden uprisings like those of the Peasant Revolt of 1381, or the earlier Town and Gown Riots of St. Scholastica's Day at Oxford in 1354, forcibly present to the designer's mind. It conceals behind its dark grey stone wall, with the narrowest slits possible for light, the slaughter-house, the brewhouse, the porter's lodge, and what was once the granary. The first three are still as they were, though used for other purposes or none.

Outer Gate stands at the east end of these buildings, a vaulted gate-house of two stories, with a turret at the west, supported outside by two massive buttresses. In the centre of the upper story in a niche is the figure of the Virgin, crowned, with the Child in her arms. On the ground floor is the porter's lodge. The two-leaved door is original, and on the right and left are two stone basins projecting from the wall, possibly holy-water stoups.

Above Outer Gate were the chambers of the steward of the college manors, now the office of his successor the bursar. Outer Court is said to have been originally open for its whole length of 200 ft., till it was curtailed by the erection in 1663 of a screen of two open stone archways at the west end, cutting off about a third of it. Offices, now pulled down, were placed here over the Lorteburn. There are indications, however, that these offices were not then erected for the first time. A more serious curtailment was caused by the erection of the warden's lodgings, begun in 1565. The beautiful carved wood mantelpiece in the warden's study is dated 1615. The gallery, the front of which looks on Outer Court, was rebuilt in 1832 by warden Barter. It was for some time used as an examination hall, and since 1910 is the Fellows' Library. It is 54 ft. long by 10 ft. wide and 11½ ft. high, and was intended seemingly for a portrait gallery and ante-room. In the warden's garden the ruins of St. Elizabeth's College are said to be traceable in very dry weather, as are those of its dependent chapel, St. Stephen, in St. Stephen's Mead by Gunner's Hole, the college bathing-place.

Middle Gate is another two-storied tower. On both its outer and inner face are groups of the Annunciation, with the angel Gabriel on the right and a much perished figure of the founder kneeling on the left. Middle Gate opens to Chamber Court, which, except for the substitution of a square 15th-century tower for the spire of Wykeham's time, is original. In Middle Gate were the warden's lodgings, including Election Chamber, so-called because until about ten years ago the elections to New College and Winchester took place there. The scholars lived in six chambers on the ground floor, three on each side, now used as day studies only.

Nine of the ten fellows occupied the rooms above first, second and third chambers, three in each room. Above fifth chamber were the ten commoners in college, and above sixth chamber, always assigned to the prefect of hall, the head of the school, were the informator or head master, the hostiarius, usher or second master, and, presumably, the tenth fellow. The sixteen choristers were in a seventh chamber, behind Sixth, now part of a new scholars' chamber called Thule. Above them were the three hired chaplains (conductitii or 'conducts,' as they are still called at Eton) and the three chapel clerks. The second master's house now absorbs the chaplains' chamber, upper Fifth and Sixth, to which additions were made at the back in the early part of the 16th century. The dining-room is a panelled room containing the portraits of noblemen who were Commoners in 1730–1.

The fellows' chambers became in 1870 the scholars' sleeping chambers and bath-rooms, 'Fourth' being now a change room.

Middle Gate looks south on chapel and school, with hall above it, while on the right is the flight of stairs to hall. Next to it is the kitchen, formerly with a projecting conduit or covered bath-room, now marked only by a tap and a stone trough.

Chapel, hall and the original school under it are of wrought stone, the rest of the quadrangle being of flint, with stone mullions and quoins, and originally roofed with 'healing' stones or stone slates. Unfortunately the eastern side was reroofed in modern days with grey Welsh slates.

Chapel measures 93 ft. by 27 ft. The roof alone, a beautiful early specimen of incipient fan vaulting, is intact. The old walls remain, but stripped of all ornament
.

In 1821–8 the splendid old glass, for the preservation of the 'sumptuous work' of which Wykeham in his statutes forbade dancing, wrestling and other disorderly games in chapel, hall or cloisters, was replaced by modern and inferior copies. At the east end is a large 'Jesse' window. Our Lady, crowned and with the Child, is the chief and the most beautiful figure, alike in colour and in drawing. The small scenes at the bottom contain figures of Edward III and Richard II, the kings under whom the college was begun and finished, Wykeham kneeling to the Virgin, and the chief mason or architect, William Winford; Wykeham's man of business, Simon Membury, an old Wykehamist, treasurer of Wolvesey and surveyor of the works, and the chief carpenter. Fortunately a considerable portion of these and of the figure of the Virgin are of old glass. The eight side windows, four on each side, containing local, mediaeval and biblical saints, are all new. Their inferiority to the old may be gauged by a visit to the original figures of St. John the Evangelist, Sephonias (the prophet Zephaniah) and St. Jacobus (James the Less) now put together in a window in the South Kensington Museum.

Further havoc was committed in 1874–5 by William Butterfield. The walls were stripped of the panelled wainscoting put up in 1636, the mediaeval brasses were torn up from the floor of the ante-chapel whither Warden Nicholas had removed them when he paved the chapel with black-and-white marble in 1681, and cast away to be lost or stolen, while for the old stalls and benches, ranged collegiate-wise north and south, there were substituted yellow pews facing eastwards, the choir being raised on an elevated dais towards the east end. The only improvement effected was the restoration of the old reredos of 1470, which had been covered by the 17th-century wainscot. It has since been filled with statues representing a mixed company, of whom William of Wykeham and Alfred the Great are the most appropriate. The old brasses on the floor have been reproduced from rubbings taken by Dr. Edwin Freshfield, solicitor to the Bank of England, when he was a boy in Commoners. They are those of Wardens Morris (Morrys), who died 1413; Thurburn, died 1450; John White, afterwards Bishop of Winchester, died 1559; John Bedell, Mayor of Winchester, formerly scholar, died 1498; and the fellows, John Willinghale, 1432; Nicholas North, 1445; Thomas Lyrypyn, 1509; and John Barnack, 1524. There is also a brass to George Ridding, head master 1866–84, and then Bishop of Southwell, died 1904.

Chapel was originally divided into the choir and ante-chapel by a rood-screen, still marked by the door giving access to it and a blind window on the south side. It took twelve days' labour to take it down in 1571–2. South-west of it in an annexe was Warden Thurburn's chantry, erected in 1450. In 1475 it was converted into the ground floor of the beautiful square, four-pinnacled tower then substituted for Wykeham's tower and spire. Unfortunately the piles on which the tower was built were not strong enough to support the additional weight. Five years after it was finished a buttress had to be built against its southern face. After the Reformation Thurburn's chantry was thrown into the chapel by piercing the wall with two arches; the column between them had to be repaired in 1671; in 1740 iron ties were introduced and in 1772 an interior buttress was erected. But after a time the structure became so unsafe that the bells could not be rung. In 1860 the whole tower was taken down, a cement foundation was inserted and the stones having been numbered it was rebuilt stone by stone as a memorial to Wardens Barter and Williams. The stone bosses in Thurburn's chantry were carefully replaced. They are of considerable interest for their canting or punning arms of four distinguished Wykehamists of the day; Thurburn himself, a flaming censer (thuribulum); Bekynton, Bishop of Bath and Wells, a beacon on a tun; Thomas Chaundler, warden of Winchester, a capital T and candles in saltire; Hugh Sugar, treasurer, then chancellor of Wells, three sugar loaves. The chapel is to be restored, the floors brought down to the old level, and the walls panelled with oak.

In the passage to cloisters, misnamed ante-chapel, is a monument in the early English style, erected in 1858 to thirteen Wykehamists who fell in the Crimean war, whence the passage itself is now called Crimea. It bears the following apposite inscription: 'Think upon them thou who art passing by to-day, child of the same family, bought by the same Lord, keep thy foot when thou goest into this house of God, then watch thine armour and make thyself ready by prayer to fight and to die, the faithful soldier and servant of Christ and of thy country.' Just beyond the end of the passage is a graceful gateway leading to School Court, erected in memory of Sir Herbert Stewart, the hero of Abu Klea, and simply inscribed 'In Memoriam Herberti Stewart.'

The cloisters, with their original Purbeck stone slates, are perhaps the most absolutely untouched of all the buildings. No cobweb or dirt defiles their oaken roofs. The thirty-six unglazed three-light windows are most beautiful. In summer Cloisters were used in the 17th century as an alternative school, whence the name of Cloister Time is still given to the summer term. Cloisters are hung with many brasses and memorial tablets. The tomb of Richard Dene, head master, who died 28 May 1494, is in the south-west corner, bereft of the brass and inscription, which Anthony Wood copied.

In the centre of Cloisters stands Chantry, the chantry of John Fromond, steward of the college, erected by him before 1426. It is a two-storied building, with a turret staircase at the south-west end. Outside may be seen carved figures of the woodward and other officials over whom the founder as steward presided, including also the bread-butler with trencher and knife, and the beer-butler with a lagena or 'black-jack.' It is 36 ft. long by 18 ft. broad and 28 ft. high in the chapel on the ground floor. The upper chamber, 14 ft. 6 in. high, originally the chantry priest's dwelling, was till 1910 a library of ancient books. The lower, which from 1629 to 1875 was also a library, is now a junior chapel. Its east window contains some fine old glass taken from Thurburn's chantry, but not originally there, as it was described as ancient glass when bought in 1483. The modern west window, given by Chief Justice Earle in 1874, contains the portraits and arms of Henry VI and others. The bosses in the roof bear the arms of the original contributors to the building. The reredos was given by Dr. Edwin Freshfield. The four side windows and statues of St. Michael and St. Gabriel were given by Archdeacon Fearon, head master 1884–1901. The brass of the first chantry priest, William Clyff, who died 24 March 1434–5, has been recently removed from Cloisters and replaced on the south wall.

The Hall is structurally intact. It measures 62 ft. by 29 ft. and is 40 ft. high to the underside of the tie-beam of the roof. The tables and forms date from the time of Elizabeth. It contains a panel portrait of William of Wykeham, perhaps painted before 1480, as it shows Winchester College with the original spire. It was bought in 1597 for £4 12s. 6d. There are also portraits of wardens from Bilson (1580–96) to Barter (1832–61), brought from the Warden's Gallery.

The original School below, now called Seventh Chamber, is no longer the great hall (magna domus) of Wykeham's time. When the present 'School' was built in 1687 Seventh Chamber Passage was cut out of its east end, which deprived it of one of its three windows, while of the four oaken columns or 'posts' which supported it only one now remains. The triple rows of stone seats on which the Prefects sat exist in the two remaining windows. Before the passage was taken out the School measured 46 ft. by 29 ft.

On the west side of Chamber Court is Kitchen, the most magnificent apartment in the place next to Hall itself. The lobby adjoining contains the far famed figure of the Trusty Servant; a man with the ears of an ass on a pig's head, the snout of which is padlocked, while the feet are those of a stag. The right hand is held out and open, the left is loaded with a shovel, pitchfork, broom and gridiron. On his left hip hangs a sword and over his right shoulder peeps a shield. An inscription in Latin elegiacs with an English translation in heroic couplets, probably of the year 1778, gives its meaning:

> *The Trusty Servant's portrait would you see*
> *This emblematic figure well survey.*
> *The porker's snout not nice in diet shows:*
> *The padlock shut no secrets he'll disclose*
> *Patient the ass his master's rage will bear,*
> *Swiftness in errand the stag's feet declare.*
> *Loaded his left hand apt to labour saith,*
> *The vest his neatness, open hand his faith.*
> *Girt with his sword, his shield upon his arm,*
> *Himself and master he'll protect from harm.*

The Trusty Servant is mentioned in the Bursar's Account for 1619 and in the account for 1628 is a payment to 'Jerome the painter for repairing the portrait of the founder in the hall and of the servant before the kitchen.'

In the Chasteau de Labur of Grignon, published in 1499, translated by Alexander Barclay about 1502 (ed. A. W. Pollard, Roxburgh Club), are some verses of advice to servants, which begin:

> *If that thou wylte thy mayster please*
> *Thou must have thre propretees,*
> *Fyrst must thou have an asses eares*
> *With an hertes fete in all degrees*
> *An hogges snoute*

which he then goes on to explain as in the writing on the wall. As Alexander Barclay was beneficed in Hampshire about this time, it is quite probable that the picture was derived from his book and was one of the ornaments which Archbishop Warham, the most prominent old Wykehamist of his day, bestowed on the college at this time. A similar figure is also described by Gilbertus Cognatus in De Officio Famulorum (Paris 1535) and by John James Hofmann in his Lexicon Universelle (1698).

'School,' standing in what was formerly a Ball Court, was built in 1687. It measures 78 ft. by 35 ft. inside and is perhaps the finest and largest school in England. It has been attributed to Sir Christopher Wren, but as it is not mentioned among his works in the Parentalia, nor are any designs for it in the collection of his plans preserved at All Souls College, the probability is that he was not the architect. The bronze statue of Wykeham over the door was given in 1692 by Caius Gabriel Cibber.

Mackenzie Walcott thus describes the interior in 1848: 'Wainscotting covers the walls as high as the sill of the deeply-embayed windows. Fronting the entrance is a tall wooden bookcase, once filled; to the right is a tier of seats, occupied at Commoners' speaking by the warden, sub-warden and head-master, ordinarily by the latter, flanked by two Wykehamical rods; on the left is the chair of the second master; on the north side of the school, facing these seats, are the chairs of the lower masters.

Against the east and west walls are built up three tiers of fixed seats, gradually rising one above the other, and extending along the whole breadth of the room; upon these the forms sit when "up at books." Along the room are set four parallel ranges of oak benches, intersected north and south by a central passage; upon them are placed the scobs (box spelt backwards), twenty-five inches long, twelve inches deep, and eighteen inches in width; the upper lid being raised as a shelter; a second cover serves the purpose of a desk; below it are kept books and implements for writing.'

The ceiling with its rich cornice is the most striking feature of the interior. It is carved with garlands and adorned with the arms of the principal contributors to the building.

On the east wall hung the Tabula Legum Paedagogicarum. This table of school laws, dating probably from the 15th century, was re-edited by Bishop Huntingford between 1773 and 1798. The laws are divided into six chapters:—I. Chapel; II. School; III. Hall; IV. Court, Town and Hills (In atrio, oppido et ad montes); V. Chambers; VI. Everywhere and Always (In omni loco et tempore). The original laws were brought from the old schoolroom.

On the west wall a huge tablet contains the famous jingle Aut disce, aut discede, manet sors tertia caedi. Above Aut disce are the rewards of learning, the mitre and crozier; above Aut discede the resort of those who departed, the sword and the pen and ink-horn; while above Manet sors tertia caedi, the last word of which is in large letters, 'the third lot to be flogged,' is the 'bibling rod.' The lines and probably the emblems were on the wall of the old school.

Meads, the ancient playground, is inclosed by a wall the highest and oldest part of which, including 'Non licet Gate' (an ancient name for this gate), was built of rubble and flint with a tiled roof in Wykeham's time. The rest of the wall is of squared stone, and was erected from the ruins of St. Elizabeth's College and the Carmelite friary in the reign of Edward VI. At the south end the walls are carved with little excavations called Temples, which were used for illuminations with the ends of candles on the last night before the Christmas holidays.

None of the other buildings of the school except Sick House are ancient. The old Sustern Hospital, Commoners' College, or 'Old Commoners,' was wholly pulled down and rebuilt in 1844, and not on the same lines, though the general idea of two quadrangles was preserved. The head master's house, built of flint and stone in the Gothic style of the period, abuts on the road called College Street. Moberly Court, which used to contain commoner prefects' studies on the west wall, is now a garden plot, with the offices of the head master's house on the west. It measures 130 ft. by 54 ft., but is wider at the southern end than at the northern. The east side of the court is formed by the west wall of the college and the second master's house. The south side is now filled by Sixth Book class-room and the masters'—formerly commoner prefects'—common room below, with Moberly Library, commonly called Mob. Lib., formerly dormitories, called Cloisters, a name transferred from the old building, above. From it two wings run out southwards, forming another quadrangle. The west side used to be called Grubbing Hall, being commoners' dining-room, and that on the east used to be called Mugging Hall, being their study and preparation room. Each was 65 ft. 4 in. long by 26 ft. 4 in. broad. Above each were long bedrooms called East and West Galleries, also a name imported from the Sisters' Hospital, and, as has been seen, from college parlance of Elizabethan days. There is not, and never was, any south side to this quadrangle, which is called Flint Court, from the flints which pave it. It is 98 ft. long by 49 ft. broad. At the bottom of Flint Court is Grass Court (about 200 ft. long), now part of Meads, but which until 1857 or thereabouts was cut off from School Court by a line of outhouses, and from Meads by a brick wall. Commoners then had no access to Meads, except on special occasions.

At the west side of Grass Court are the Fives Courts and War Gate (built as a South African War memorial in 1902), the usual mode of access to Meads and college for Commoners. Beyond the gate are Racquet Court and Gymnasium, which are masked by Museum, a building of considerable architectural pretensions in red brick with yellow stone arches in the rococo Renaissance style, erected to commemorate the Quincentenary celebration held in 1893. A few yards farther on is Sick House, formerly standing in its own grounds called Sick House Meads, and still separated by a hedge and a small garden from the rest of Meads. It is a charming little house with no great pretensions, in red brick with white stone quoins and mullions. It was built in 1640 by Warden Harris, who called it 'Bethesda,' which name is inscribed in Hebrew characters over the door, while in Latin is also written 'Sumtibus Harrisii fuit aedificata Bethesda.' The back part was added or enlarged by John Taylor, a Fellow in 1775. A huge red brick infirmary, erected in 1893, occupies the south part of the old Sick House Meads.

Beyond Meads Wall, on the right of Lavender Meads, are the new Science Schools built in 1903, and, invisible behind them in Culverlea, Music School, dating from the same year.

At the farthest end of New Field is Webbe Tent, a picturesque thatched cricket pavilion, erected in 1887 and dedicated to the memory of H. R. Webbe, captain of 'Lords' in 1875, by his brother, the wellknown Harrow cricketer, A. J. Webbe.

The plate consists of two chalices and paten covers of 1611; two patens, the gift of Warden Nicholas and his wife in 1683; another paten of 1833 given by will of John Johnson, D.D.; two flagons of 1627, given by Warden Love in 1629; an alms-dish of 1681 also given by Warden Nicholas in that year; and a secular cup of late 16th or early 17th-century workmanship, inscribed 'D. D. Gul. Master in Usum Sacristae Coll. Winton, 1762.' All are of silver-gilt.

The plate of Fromond's chantry in the college cloisters consists of a silver chalice, paten, flagon, eucharistic spoon and alms-plate, the first four dated 1895, the latter 1894. They are engraved 'The gift of Confrère Edwin Freshfield of the Order of St. John of Jerusalem in England.' The altar linen in use in the chantry was also given by Dr.

Edwin Freshfield and comprises some very beautiful lace, mostly of Greek workmanship.

Remains of the Carmelite friary have been found near the College Sick House and Memorial Buildings in Meads and in the gardens at the back of the houses north of the memorial gateway on the east side of Kingsgate Street. To the south of Garnier Road, which forms the southern boundary of 'The Riddings,' as Lower College Meads are called, nearly opposite the old graveyard of St. Faith, is Prior's Barton House marking the site of the manor of Prior's Barton. In the meadows still further south again of the college in the old suburb of Sparkford is the hospital of St. Cross (vide infra).

On the summit of St. Catherine's Hill are a bank and ditch, within which the foundations of St. Catherine's chapel are said to exist, but there is no masonry now showing. Near the clump of trees on the top is a maze cut in the turf, within a square. It is said to have been made by the college boy who wrote 'Dulce Domum,' but nothing seems to be known of its actual origin.

As the college is still in full occupation and many of the buildings are the originals that have been built, refurbished, repurposed and merged over the years since the college's founding, there is very little in the way of archaeology for this site relating to the college's many transformations. The Carmelite friary and the other buildings found in the Meads being the exception.

Chapter 5 Winchester's Jewish past

Early Medieval Jewish Winchester

Winchester has an important Jewish past. The earliest record of people of the Jewish faith being resident in Winchester dates to the mid twelfth century (1148), making it one of the earliest Jewish communities in England outside London. It was also one of the largest and wealthiest Jewish communities in England at the time. Jewish merchants were invited into England in around 1070 by William The Conqueror to act as financiers and traders, there is a plaque on a wall in a passageway off Winchester High Street commemorating this fact. They mostly based themselves in London but gradually they moved to the areas where there was a perceived need for their services.

The Christian doctrine at the time did not allow for the lending of money for interest or usury. The new testament forbade this action but this did not affect Jews as their religious book, the Tanakh/Torah, is based on the books of the old testament. The Jews lent money to the King, the church and to Winchesters merchants. There was no shortage of customers for these loans and a great many of the people wanting the loans would have been partly based in Winchester as this was the centre of the royal dynasty and had been since Saxon times as well as all the people who served the royal household. The nobles needed to finance the building of their castles or rebuild them in stone after initially building them out of wood, they needed to maintain their control over their serfs and other subjects and these strong statements in the landscape reminded everyone who the boss was.

There were the churches and monastic orders also, who were all represented within the city and were looking to expand across the country with their more substantial, stone built, churches replacing the earlier wooden ones. These needed to be impressive to reinforce their place in subjugating the populace. The many merchants also looked to the Jews to finance their expansion, many based in the trading ports of the south coast, but who looked to Winchester for this service as it was the key administrative centre.

The Jewish community of Winchester is one that was important to Winchesters development as a central administrative city as well as a base for the royal house and its attendants during the Norman and Plantagenet periods. It is celebrated in several street names like Jewry Street. It was around the area of Jewry Street that the Winchester Jewish community was based, this being in the north west of the medieval city.

Here there were houses, tenements, store rooms, a school and a synagogue. Not all the Jews that settled in Winchester were the rich merchants, they also brought in their skilled artisans which were an integral part of the community. Winchester appears to have been very tolerant of its Jewish community at a time when other areas of England were not.

The Winchester Jews escaped the pogroms of 1189-90 that so afflicted other towns such as London and York after a number of the principal Jews of England presented themselves to do homage to Richard I, when he was crowned at Westminster. There appears to have been a superstition against Jews being admitted to such a holy ceremony, and they were upset and in many cases angry. The false rumour was spread from Westminster to the City of London that the king had ordered a

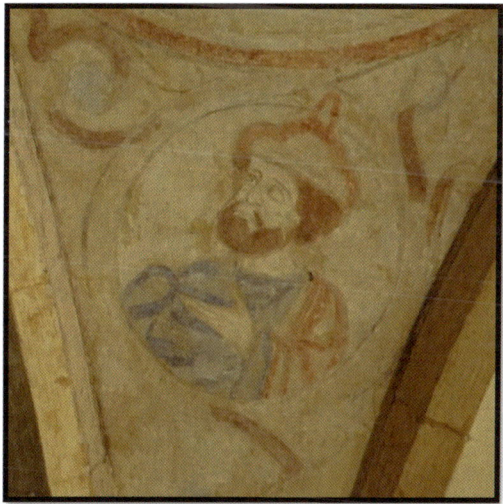

Jewish Figure Holy Sepulchre Chapel Winchester Cathedral ©Stephen Old

massacre of the Jews and the anti-Semitic found vent for their prejudices.

However in Winchester a much more tolerant attitude was taken, an indication or mark of the depth of involvement of Jews in commercial life maybe. Between the street they occupied, Jewry Street and the present Royal Oak Passage, a synagogue and a Jewish school were built and they were granted permission to bury their dead just outside the city on land within the Priory of St Swithun. The initial act that allowed the Jews to settle in England only allowed them to be buried in one cemetery and this was located in London.

The special relationship that existed between the Christian church and the Jews is illustrated in Winchester cathedral's Holy Sepulchre Chapel, where Jews feature in some wall paintings dating to around 1160. They are identifiable as Jews by their conical, pointed, and funnel-shaped hats. There is also a carved Star of David in the choir stalls, though it is unknown as to the significance of this carving and its location. Quite often the carvers were given free rein over their designs, could this have been carved by a Jewish artisan? Through the many centuries, these Jewish represensations have survived in this

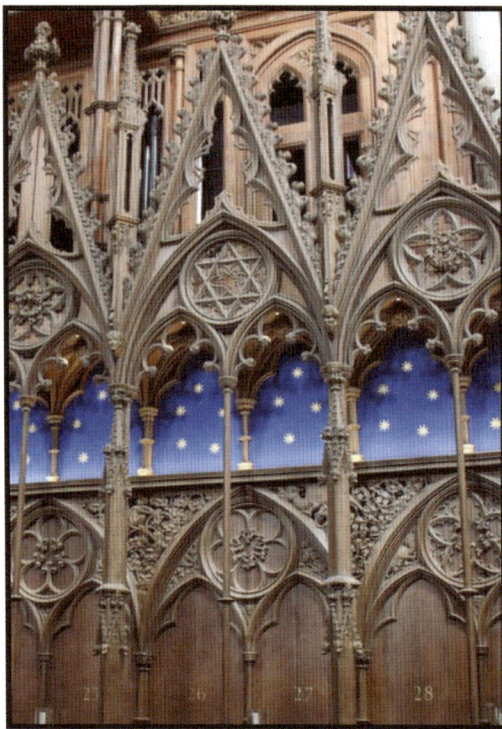

Choir Stall Winchester Cathedral with Star of David motif ©Stephen Old

most christian of holy places. This is an anomoly that may never be fully explained.

Richard of Devizes, writing in 1190 stated that "Winchester is for the Jews the Jeruslaem of that land (England); here alone they enjoy perpetual peace." This suggests that Winchester had a reputation as a safe place for Jews. This also I think alludes to the fact that there was now a cemetery for Jews in Winchester, where they could bury their dead and perform their burial rites.

Their role in the administrative matters of the city has been well recorded in many of the rolls and chirographs (multi part financial record and legal documents) of financial transactions in the city. Within the Castle was the "Jews Tower" which was a designated place of safety or refuge for the Jews of Winchester in case of trouble. It is not recorded that this facility was used in 1265 when Simon de Montfort the younger, who sacked Winchester's Jewish Quarter, killing any Jew that did not make it to the refuge of the tower.

Notable Jews in Winchester include Isaac the chirographer and Chera his wife. There was also the Jewess Licoricia, whose extensive business dealings eventually brought about her murder. Her murder was probably part of an attempted robbery. Licoricia was buried in the Jewish cemetery which was located outside the city walls, this was found during excavation in 1995 at the junction of Crowder Terrace and Mews Lane.

Her second husband was David of Oxford, another one of Winchesters prominent merchants. Licoricia first appears as a young widow with four children, three sons and a daughter and she went on to have another son with David of Oxford before his death two years after they were married.

Like most Jews at this time, Licoricia lived under the protection of King Henry III, but as a payoff was expected to provide the King with any funds he might require.

Isaac of Newbury, another Jewish wool merchant lived on Jewry Street which looked a little different in medieval times; originally called Scowrterne stret (Shoemakers Street), it was a busy area with many properties, traders and workshops. It was close to the castle and the Jews Tower.

Also on Jewry Street there was a property of Abraham and Jaceus who held land from the abbot of Hyde Abbey until 1290, demonstrating that Jews had close business connections with the church. Another property on Jewry Street was sold by Isaac of Southwark to William de Seleborn in 1280; Seleborn (Selbourne) priory was part financed by loans from Winchester's Jews.

Just to the east of Jewry Street was where the medieval synagogue (scola) was located. The scola was in the courtyard of a property owned by Abraham Pinch (son of Chera, a female money-lender). Pinch was an active usurer, and this made him unpopular. He was accused of murdering a child, and although the child's mother was guilty of that crime, Pinch was accused of theft and so he was executed for that instead. Pinch was buried beneath the gallows erected in this street opposite the scola, specifically for the purpose of hanging him.

On David of Oxford's death in 1244, Licoricia was imprisoned in the Tower of London until she promised to pay death duties of 5,000 marks. This was an enormous sum of money, part of this money was put towards financing the building of the shrine to Edward the Confessor in Westminster Abbey. A mark weighed 8 ounces in silver and was worth a little over 13 shillings. A knight earned about 2 shillings a day and a kitchen servant about 2 shillings a year.

By the latter part of the 13th century the situation had worsened for the Jews in Winchester, many of them trying to leave the city before all their goods could be confiscated. It was all coming to a head, The English establishment in the form of the King and the church had made full use of the Jews ability to finance their ambitious schemes, but now, probably because they could not meet the repayments, the Jews were hounded and eventually expelled.

One of the most distinguished of these Jews who were exiting Winchester, was a man called Benedict. He became a Guildsman of the city in 1268, an amazing feat of achievement for a Jew at that time and he went on to buy property all over Winchester. He was an extremely wealthy man who lent money to many prominent Hampshire families, including the notorious knight come highwayman Adam de Gurdon and to ecclesiastical men, abbots and priors.

Licoricia and David of Oxfords son, Duceman (also known as 'Asher' and 'Sweteman') was a wool merchant who held several properties in Winchester, one of which was located on what is now the western end of the High Street.

Another key player in Winchester at the time was Samme, a converted Jew. A small number of Jews in Winchester converted to Christianity; one was Henry of Winchester. Henry acted for the king in 1275 when usury (the main source of income for England's Jews) became illegal. Because the work Jews were allowed to do was limited, the community sometimes turned to coin clipping; a crime that carried the death sentence. Henry travelled around England noting the names of coin clippers, and in 1279, 269 Jews and 29 Christians were executed for this offense. One man hanged for coin-clipping was Benedict, son of Licoricia, and step-brother to Duceman.

In a move that was later seen in Nazi Germany in the mid-20th century, in 1253 it became a requirement for all Jews over the age of 7 years to wear a yellow felt patch, six inches by three inches, that was shaped like two stone tablets, like those given to Moses on Mount Sinai. This marked out Jews everywhere for further persecution and made life in England for Jews very difficult. How this played out in Winchester can only be guessed at. Were the citizens of Winchester still as tolerant and accepting? Certainly at the higher levels of Winchester society this attitude seemed to have changed.

The trickle of persecution of the Jews in Winchester, sapped the city of its financial muscle, the loss of the community in 1290, when the Jews were expelled from England by royal decree of King Edward I, dated the 18th July, with a date of the 1st of November (All Saints Day) for completion, playing a major part in the decline of the city of Winchester at that time, as it owed so much of its wealth and prosperity to its Jewish community.

There is now very little evidence left in Winchester of this vibrant and, at the time, vitally important religious and artisan community. There is not currently a synagogue in Winchester and the last Jewish Community was active only during World War Two (1939-1945) when refugees from the war in Europe were settled here. During their stay they were an integral part of the wider Winchester community and it's war effort.

Archaeology and Architecture

As previously stated, there is very little evidence left of the Jewish presence in Winchester, on the surface or underground. Archaeological excavations carried out on the Jewish cemetery, especially the 1995 dig at Mews Lane and Crowder Terrace (southern end of the cemetery) , which produced 88 burials, has shown that the majority of Jews that lived and died in Winchester were not the rich financiers and merchants but the ordinary people.

This located the Jewish Cemetery just outside the city walls to the north west, the area now to the west of the railway line and would have abutted the castle walls. The cemetery would have been greatly disturbed by the building of the railway in Victorian times. Of the 88 burials, only 73 could be aged and 49 of these were infants, the total split being six adults, seven adolescent, eleven children (6-10) and 49 infants. This might show that, as at York Jewish Cemetery, the burials were zoned with infant burials being placed at the peripheral areas.

In 2017 a fund was started to pay for and get commissioned a statue to commemorate the role of Licoricia, to be placed on a plinth near to Winchester Discovery Centre on Jewry Street. The design shows Licoricia in medieval dress with her young son Asher slightly behind her. At the time of writing, the statue was in place but the expected official unveiling by Prince Charles was postponed due to Prince Charles contracting Covid.

The statue was visited by Prince Charles on March 3rd 2022 when he also officially opened the refurbished ARC building. The statue will be used to educate and promote tolerance and is seen as a key addition to this conservation area and an asset that will help celebrate Winchester's long association with diverse communities.

The plinth has the quotation "Love thy neighbour as thyself" which is written in both English and Hebrew. This is a phrase found in some form in Judaism, Christianity and Islam so can be a true, uniting and inclusive saying and very apt.

Statue of Licoricia and Asher, ARC Winchester ©Stephen Old

Bishop of Winchester, Samuel Wilberforce (1805-1873, in post 1870-1873) was a prolific writer of religious texts, books of sermons and history books, but one of his enduringly popular books is his "Heroes of Hebrew History" which he wrote in 1870 when he was resident in Winchester as the newly appointed Bishop. Did he write this book in response to learning of the history of the Jewish community that was once so important to the city's economy and daily life?

Definitions

The Jewish world is different from the Christian world and its religious practices are also very different, though they have the same origins. This being the case, there are different items within the Jewish place of worship to what can be seen in a Christian church. They also retain their traditional names, which to non-Jewish people can seem strange. I have listed a few items here with the aim to explain what these items are and their use within Jewish religious ceremonies, this is not an exhaustive list.

Ark – or Ark of the Covenant, the wooden chest which contained the tablets of the laws of the ancient Israelites. Carried by the Israelites on their wanderings in the wilderness, it was later placed by Solomon in the Temple at Jerusalem. Each Synagogue will have a representation of the Ark of the Covenant is a cupboard where the Torah scrolls are stored.

Ark Wall – A decorated wall against which the Ark is placed within the Synagogue.

Aron Hakodesh – This is another name for the cupboard where the Torah scrolls are kept.

Banca – this is the canopied warden's pew which is usually against a side wall near to the Tebah (Tevah). There is only one example known to exist in Britain and that is at Bevis Marks Synagogue in London.

Beit K'nesset – Another name for the Synagogue, in Hebrew it means "meeting place".

Bimah – This is the platform and table, centrally placed in the synagogue and used for the Torah readings by the Rabbi.

Cantor Seats – These are the seats reserved for the Cantor(s) near to the Bimah, from where the Cantor can lead the congregation in singing.

Echal – Another name for the large decorated cupboard where the Ark and Torah are kept.

Kippah – This is the skull cap that all men have to wear when in a synagogue or attending a meeting or ceremony that is part of the Jewish tradition.

Menorah – This is a candelabrum usually of seven branches, used in Jewish worship. An eight branched one is used at Hanukkah, often achieved by adding an extra branch using a socket in the front of the seven branched version. There is also a nine branch version.

Mikveh – This is a bath or plunge pool used for the purification in some Jewish ceremonies.

Ner Tamid – This is a large and elaborate lamp that often hangs over the Bimah, it is a lamp that is never extinguished and Ner Tamid means "eternal light" in Hebrew.

Rabbi's Chairs – These are the chairs placed by the Bimah for the Rabbis where they can sit waiting for their part of the ceremonies.

Scola/Shul – These are alternative words for the Synagogue and literally means a school, which is traditionally part of the synagogues function.

Sifrei Torah – This is the box that holds the Torah scrolls and is covered in an elaborate embroidered cloth.

Synagogue - Synagogues are consecrated spaces used for the purpose of prayer, reading of the Tanakh (the entire Hebrew Bible, including the Torah), study and assembly; however, a synagogue is not necessary for Jewish worship. Synagogues have a place for prayer (the main sanctuary) and may also have rooms for study, a social hall, and offices. Some have a separate room called a Beth Midrash, which means "house of study".

Tanakh - The Hebrew Bible or Tanach , is the canonical collection of Hebrew scriptures, including the Torah. These texts are almost exclusively in Biblical Hebrew, with a few passages in Biblical Aramaic.

Tebah/Tevah – This is another word for the Ark where the Torah Scrolls are kept and comes from the Hebrew for the Ark that Noah built.

Torah/Torah Scrolls – This is the first five books of the Hebrew Bible Genesis, Exodus, Leviticus, Numbers and Deuteronomy.

Yarmulke – This is the Yiddish word for the Kippah or skull cap.

Chapter 6 Pre-Christian Winchester

The key factors that have made Winchester a desirable place to settle have been the same throughout history and were probably recognised as far back as the Neolithic or even earlier. Fertile soils, good water supply, protective hills are all key elements. The evidence for domesticity from the Neolithic through the Bronze Age and onto the Iron Age is sparse, but evidence of this area being occupied during this time is strong. The finding of burials, the frequent turning up of stone tools, all point to this areas importance.

Iron Age

The wider area around Winchester has been inhabited for a long time, with three Iron Age hillforts, Oram's Arbour, St. Catherine's Hill, and Worthy Down all close by, as well as other evidence. In the Late Iron Age, an urban settlement type developed, known as an oppidum, although the archaeology of this phase remains obscure.

This settlement became an important centre for the British Belgae tribe; however, it still remains unclear how the Belgae came to control this initial settlement. Caesar recorded that the tribe had crossed the channel as raiders (probably in the 1st century BCE), only to later establish themselves. The Roman account of continental invaders has been challenged in recent years with scientific studies favouring a gradual change through increased trade links rather than migration. This is backed up by the continuing trade with the continent that Winchester has enjoyed all through the middle ages.

To the Celtic Britons, the settlement was likely known as Wentā or Venta (from a common Celtic word meaning "tribal town" or "meeting place"). Although an etymology connected with the Celtic word for "white" (Modern Welsh gwyn) has also been suggested, due to Winchester's situation upon chalk. It was the Latinised versions of this name, together with that of the tribe that gave the town its Roman name of Venta Belgarum.

Evidence for specific religious observance from this period is scant, but it is known that the Belgae were a manifestation of a cultural-religious movement that was the expression of the Celtic war-band culture that sought to glorify their main god "Belenos" who they saw as their version of Apollo or Alexander. At this time there was no written Celtic language so we rely on Roman written accounts and the archaeological evidence from the period of co-existence.

Roman Period

After the Roman conquest of Britain in 43 CE, the settlement occupied by the Belgae tribe served as their capital (Latin: civitas) and was distinguished as Venta Belgarum, "Venta of the Belgae". Although in the early years the Roman occupation it was of subsidiary importance to both Silchester and Chichester, Venta developed to eclipse them both by the latter half of the second century. At the beginning of the third century, Winchester was given protective stone walls. At around this time the city covered an area of 144 acres (58 hectares), making it among the largest towns in Roman Britain by surface area. There was a limited suburban area outside the walls. Like many other Roman towns however, Winchester began to decline in the later fourth century prior to the withdrawal of the Roman support in 410CE.

As a key provincial Roman town, there would have been shrines and temples erected for the worshipping of the Roman and local deities. Evidence for this is found both in literature and in the archaeological remains that have been excavated and examined so far. The main evidence for religious observance in this period comes from the study of the burial practices and how they changed over time. The change from pagan to Christian interment, the rise and decline of cremations, the placement of grave goods and move away from them, are all indications that the underlying religious base to society was changing throughout this period. Evidence gathered from just the Lankhills Roman cemetery alone indicates the changes seen in burial practices over time.

What form these religious practices took can only be guessed at using a combination of the Roman written word and the archaeological evidence. Evidence of any Roman temples in Winchester is sparse with more hopefully to be found but it can be assumed that they would follow the general trend across the empire. The main underlying religion was the usually the cult of the emperor, the living god, but on top of this each wave of new people from across the empire would have brought their own religious practices. At military sites across Britain, Mithraism spread quickly and was also taken up within the general population.

The only Roman temple uncovered so far in Winchester was found in the excavations on Lower Brook Street run by Martin Biddle. It was dated to around 100 CE and was of the Romano-Celtic style, being a square or rectangular building in plan with a central shrine or Cella, the home of the deity, with a covered ambulatory around the outside. There is no evidence of a Classical Pantheon in Winchester, however, a town of this size would have had one. There is some evidence that leads us to believe there was one, but not where it was located. In the railway cutting was found a statue head, now thought to be of Jupiter and also a figurine of Omphale, these would have been key features of a Pantheon along with representations of other Classical gods.

Many cults would have made an appearance in Winchester during this period, many were based on Celtic myths , some on Roman myths but many also on a combination, merging the deities to create a local version. One of the cults seen in Winchester was the cult of Epona, the horse goddess, which was probably introduced via Roman cavalrymen then conflated with Rhiannon, a local British deity. Evidence of this was found in a small wooden statuette found in Lower Brook Street, near the temple site, and the discovery of two horse burials just inside the boundary of the cemetery on Victoria Road East.

Most Roman houses had small domestic shrines for the family to pray and libate at and there is a fair amount of evidence for these in Winchester with the finding of small statues of Venus and local deities. But it is with the grave goods that we get a bigger picture of the personal religious beliefs of the Roman population of Winchester, with representations seen of Jupiter, Cerberus and other items intended to act as payment to the ferryman to cross the river Styx and into the underworld. There is also evidence of a cosmic dimension to some beliefs with the finding of a small spoked copper alloy wheel, thought to be a sun symbol to represent Taranis, a Romano-British sky god.

Chapter 7 The Black Death and Winchester's Clergy

There have been several events in the history of Winchester, often shared with the rest of the country, that have had a profound effect on its population, infrastructure and general well-being. The major ones brought to mind are the retreat of the Roman Military, the Norman Invasion, the Anarchy, the Simon de Montfort attack on the Jewish community and the Dissolution of the Religious institutions under Henry VIII. The other major event, that had what looks like a disproportionate affect on the clergy of Winchester, was the "Black Death" of 1348-49.

In a study by Dr John Merriman, who looked into this event for his PhD at the University of Winchester, he shows that this was a time of great upheaval in the church. I will summarize his findings with a few additional notes.

The "Black Death" was not the first or last of the plague epidemics to affect Britain, along with the rest of Europe, there were several waves of disease that swept across the country. The "Black Death" was, however, one of the most destructive. The disease is said to have arrived in Britain at Melcombe Regis, near Weymouth, on a merchant ship, but soon took hold and spread. There is still an ongoing debate as to how the disease was spread, the traditional explanation that it was spread by the fleas on rats that came ashore from this ship has been questioned and new evidence has pointed to the carrier actually being human fleas and lice.

There is no doubt, however, that it was very quickly transmitted from person to person, village to village, town to town, with very few places remaining unaffected. A lack of understanding of how this disease was spread aided its progress, along with a general lack of general cleanliness. In charge of many of the efforts to deal with this disease were the clergy, both locally and nationally and they appear to have been unprepared for the role.

When it came to Winchester, as with other centres of religious importance, the clergy were very much the front line, very hands on with their efforts to salve the souls and repair the body of their congregation.

The church held a key position in the lives of the 14th century population of Britain. The three most important events in a persons life , baptism, marriage and burial were all overseen by the church and it is estimated that at that time 99.9% of the population were Christian believers. Furthermore, the church was responsible for carrying out public services like education, charity and healthcare.

The clergy in general were hard hit by the 1348 outbreak. Considering the public nature of their roles, urban outposts and workplace proximity, like monasteries, it is no surprise that an estimated 46.6% of the clergy nationally perished. However, Dr Merriman's study concluded that in the Winchester area, which included Hampshire, Surrey the area around the Dorset Avon, the clergy mortality rate lay at around 49.2%. The situation became so dire the Bishop of Bath and Wells, Ralph of Shrewsbury, suggested that in the absence of a priest or a man, a final confession could be made "even to a woman". It was noted that the death rate in the country areas as around 40% whilst the rate in urban areas was nearer 60% leading to an estimated population loss nationally of around 45%. Compared with the global rate of loss of around 65%, dropping from around eighty million to around thirty million, Britain was not so badly affected.

The initial impact on the church was immediate and devastating. King Edward III compensated for the amount of sudden vacancies by employing a disproportionate number of new clergymen. In 1348 207 new priests were employed, in 1349, at the height of the outbreak, this rose to 542. Whilst this solved the initial problem of numbers in place, the standard of these clergy fell. There were examples of priests who couldn't understand the order or some, even read.

The founding of Trinity College, Cambridge and New College, Oxford came about to redress these shortcomings and to ensure a reduction in intellectual poverty. It also greatly increased the speed of religious promotions as it would usually take about 17 years to become a priest. Andrew de Bokensfield waited only 8 months after becoming an acolyte. As positive effect was that mass employment broke down some of the class barriers to entering the church and the new clergy were arguably more in touch with the average man than those employed before the pandemic.

Another problem created by the plague outbreak was the rapidly increasing demand for graves. In 1349 the Winchester cemetery began to encroach upon the market place. This met with strong disapproval from the townspeople, who were taken to court by Bishop Edington, bishop of Winchester at the time, when new boundary lines were drawn.

Dr Merriman concluded that the overall effect of the "Black Death" on Winchester were a mixture of both change and continuity in the church. Whilst the clergy replenishment altered the make-up of the church's employment profile and the church in general moving forward, and improved access to scholarships, in many ways the church became more exclusive as the disease simultaneously limited reform due to the financial strain. In the immediate aftermath money was needed to rebuild the church as an institution rather than for alms, education and charity.

Chapter 8 Wrapping Up

In this book I have tried to show how important a religious life and the many religious institutions have been to the development and life of Winchester through the ages. I have tried to de-mystify the writings that made up the Victorian County Histories which were published in 1903 but which took the core of their text from previous books and articles, adding interpretations and modifying the language where appropriate to make it easier for the reader.

I have added a few additional details from the archaeology, a result of the many planned and rescue excavations carried out in Winchester over the twentieth and twenty first centuries. The full details of these excavations can be found in the many really good books written on the subject. See the bibliography for more details.

I have not written this book to be an academic text, but as a layman's guide. I hope this might inspire you to read and explore this subject to greater depths.

Bibliography

Listed here are the books I have consulted during my research.

Words from Wills and other Probate Records – Stuart A Raymond
ISBN:1860061818 Federation of Family History Societies

Winchester, An Archaeological Assessment – Patrick Ottaway
ISBN: 9781785704499 Oxbow Books

The Search for Winchester's Anglo-Saxon Minsters – Martin Biddle
ISBN:9781784918576 Archaeopress Archaeology

The Late Roman Cemetery At Lankhills, Winchetser – Paul Booth,
Andrew Simmonds, Angela Boyle, Sharon Clough, H E M Cool and
Daniel Pascoe
ISBN:9780904220629 Oxford Archaeology South

Abbeys & Priories – Glyn Coppack
ISBN: 9781848684195 Amberley Publishing

The Sutton Companion To Churches – Stephen Friar
ISBN: 0750934743 Sutton Publishing

Winchester's Anglo-Saxon Medieval and Later Suburbs – Patrick
Ottaway and Ken Qualmann
ISBN:9781999978006 Winchester Museum Service/Historic England
Reports

Nunnaminster – A Saxon and Medieval Community of Nuns – Graham
Scobie And Ken Qualmann
ISBN: 0861350146 Winchester Museum Service

An Historical Map Of Winchester – Winchester Excavations
Committee
ISBN: 9780993469817 Town & City Historical Maps

Pitkin Guide to Winchester Cathedral – Dr John Crook
ISBN: 0853728755 Pitkin Guides

Winchester Illustrated – Alan W Ball
ISBN: 1841140244 Halsgrove Publishing

A History of the County of Hampshire: Volume 2, edited by H Arthur
Doubleday and William Page (London, 1903)

The End